This edition first published in 1993 by
Sunburst Books, Deacon House, 65 Old Church Street,
London, SW3 5BS

Copyright © Editorial LIBSA, Narciso Serra, 25 – Tel 433 54 07 –
28007 MADRID
4.ª EDICION 1991
Copyright English language text © 1993 Sunburst Books

ISBN 1 85778 011 6

Printed and bound in China

FISH
AND SEAFOOD

CONTENTS

INTRODUCTION

There are hundreds of different ways of serving fish and a vast selection of different types to choose from. The recipes in the following pages range from easy-to-cook, economic family suppers, such as Sautéed Haddock and Whiting in Cheese Sauce, to sumptuous dinner party dishes, such as Champagne Turbot and Sparkling Sole. There are hot and cold dishes, and both filling winter meals and lighter, more summery recipes. Few other foods are so adaptable and so varied.

Modern transport and refrigeration processes ensure that fish reach our shops and markets in the peak of condition. Freshness is the key to both taste and nutritional value. Smell and appearance are the two main indicators of freshness. First, it should smell fresh and pleasant. The scales should be shiny and iridescent and the flesh should be firm. The eyes should be bulging and the gills damp and bright. If you are buying fish steaks, there should be no discolouration around the bone and the flesh of both steaks and fillets should be firm and pale. For the best flavour, fish should be cooked on the day it is bought and should always be kept in the refrigerator.

For the health-conscious – and the weight-conscious – fish is the ideal choice. For example, 200 g/7 oz hake fillet contains the same quantity of protein as an equal weight of sirloin steak, but has far fewer calories (150 rather than 320) because it has far less fat. Even the oiliest fish have no more fat than pork. Fish is a good source of protein and is rich in minerals such as phosphorus, iodine, iron, copper and magnesium. It provides B complex vitamins and oily fish also contains vitamins A and D.

Shellfish are also part of the sea's rich harvest. The list is mouthwatering - crab, lobster, mussels, clams, prawns, langoustines and many more. Often served cold as a starter, shellfish may also be prepared as filling, nourishing and hot main courses. Prawns and langoustines provide the perfect garnish to many other fish dishes. The seafood recipes, too, range from the simple yet delicious Dijon Mussels to that great classic of French cuisine, Lobster Thermidor.

Whether your tastes are extravagant or restrained, simple or exotic, in the following pages you are sure find some new and interesting ways of serving fish and seafood that will delight you and your family.

WHITEFISH

SOLE WITH GRAPES

Serves 4

2 sole, filleted, trimmings reserved
juice of 1 lemon
75 ml/2¹/₂ fl oz white wine
salt and freshly ground black pepper
¹/₂ tsp grated nutmeg
120 g/4 oz butter
60 g/2 oz flour
1 egg, lightly beaten
approx 75 ml/2¹/₂ fl oz milk
500 g/1 lb 2 oz Muscatel grapes, peeled,
   halved and seeded

Put the fish trimmings, lemon juice, wine, salt, pepper, nutmeg and 60 g/2 oz of the butter in a large pan. Bring to the boil and simmer for 20 minutes.

Meanwhile, coat the fillets in half the flour and beaten egg. Melt 30 g/1 oz of the remaining butter and fry the fish for 5-7 minutes on each side until golden. Reduce the heat and keep warm.

Strain and measure the fish stock. Make it up to 300 ml/10 fl oz with milk. Melt the remaining butter and stir in the remaining flour. Cook for 1 minute, stirring. Remove from the heat and gradually stir in the stock mixture. Return to the heat, bring to the boil, stirring, and simmer for 1-2 minutes, stirring. Add the grapes and cook gently for 3-4 minutes.

Arrange the sole fillets on a long serving dish, pour over the grape sauce and serve.

DEVILLED WHITING

Serves 6

1 kg/2¹/₄ lb whiting fillets
salt
¹/₂ tsp curry powder
30 g/1 oz flour
150 g/5 oz butter
200g/7 oz long-grain rice
1 tbsp chopped parsley
2 tbsp vegetable oil
500 g/1 lb 2 oz tomatoes, skinned and halved
500 g/1 lb 2 oz mushrooms, chopped

Devilled sauce:
30 g/1 oz butter
1 small onion, peeled and finely chopped
2 tsp curry paste
30 g/1 oz flour

400 ml/14 fl oz milk
1 bouquet garni
120 ml/4 fl oz cream
few drops lemon juice

Season the fish with the salt and curry powder and coat with flour. Melt 60 g/2 oz of the butter and sauté half the fillets. Keep warm while you cook the remaining fillets, adding more butter as required.

Cook the rice for 15-20 minutes in boiling salted water. Drain, rinse in boiling water, sprinkle with parsley and reserve.

To make the sauce, melt the butter and fry the onion for 5-7 minutes, until soft. Stir in the curry paste and flour and cook, stirring, for 1 minute. Remove from the heat and gradually stir in the milk. Return to the heat and bring to the boil, stirring. Add the bouquet garni and simmer for 3-4 minutes. Stir in the cream and lemon juice.

Heat 1 tbsp of the oil and sauté the tomatoes over high heat. Remove from the pan and set aside. Add the remaining oil to the frying-pan and sauté the mushrooms over high heat. Return the tomatoes to the pan, mix well and heat gently for 2-3 minutes.

Arrange the fish on a large serving dish and spoon over a little of the sauce. Garnish with the sautéed vegetables and serve with the rice. Discard the bouquet garni and serve the sauce separately.

SAUCY HADDOCK

Serves 6

1 kg/2¹/₄ lb haddock fillets
salt and freshly ground black pepper
1 tbsp vegetable oil
2 garlic cloves, peeled and finely chopped
2 large onions, peeled and finely chopped
3 tomatoes, skinned, seeded and chopped
1 tsp chopped thyme or ¹/₂ tsp dried thyme
1 bay leaf
1 tsp sugar (optional)
250 ml/9 fl oz white wine
2-3 tbsp water (optional)

Season the fish fillets and set aside in a flameproof casserole.

Heat the oil and fry the garlic and onions for 5 minutes until soft. Add the tomatoes, thyme, bay leaf and salt and cook gently for 10 minutes. If the sauce is

a little acid, add the sugar. Stir in the wine.

Pour the sauce over the fish and simmer for about 10 minutes, or until cooked through. Serve hot with chips.

SOLE WITH ROYAL SAUCE

Serves 6

3 sole, filleted
90 g/3 oz butter
salt and freshly ground black pepper
juice of 1 lemon
120 ml/4 fl oz white wine
250 g/9 oz prawns, peeled and deveined
250 g/9 oz mushrooms, chopped

Royal sauce:
30 g/1 oz butter
30 g/1 oz flour
60 g/2 oz mushrooms, finely chopped
2 egg yolks
120 ml/4 fl oz single cream
2 truffles, chopped

Preheat the oven to 190° C/375° F, gas mark 5. Fold each fillet along the middle and arrange in rings in one layer in an ovenproof casserole. Dice half the butter and dot over the fish. Season and pour over the lemon juice and white wine. Bake for 10-12 minutes, until tender.

Meanwhile, melt the remaining butter in a pan and sauté the prawns and mushrooms for 2-3 minutes.

Transfer the mushroom and prawn mixture to a serving dish and arrange the sole fillets on top. Keep hot. Reserve the cooking liquids from the mushroom and prawn mixture and from the sole.

To make the sauce, melt the butter and stir in the flour. Cook, stirring, for 1 minute. Remove from the heat and gradually stir in the reserved cooking liquids. Add the mushrooms and bring slowly to the boil, stirring. Continue cooking for 2 minutes, stirring. Remove from the heat and rub the sauce through a wire sieve. Return to gentle heat and beat in the egg yolks and cream, but do not allow to boil. Stir in the truffles.

Spoon a little of the sauce over the fish on the serving dish and serve immediately, with the remaining sauce served separately.

Top: Saucy Haddock
Bottom: Sole with Royal Sauce

SOLE WITH PRAWNS

Serves 4

1 kg/2¹/₄ lb sole fillets, trimmings reserved
120 g/4 oz prawns, peeled and deveined
170 g/6 oz butter
salt and freshly ground black pepper
1 tbsp flour
75 ml/3 fl oz white wine
3 egg yolks, lightly beaten with 1 tsp water
125 g/4 oz Mediterranean prawns

Put the fish trimmings and prawn shells in a pan with 300 ml/10 fl oz water. Cover and simmer for 30 minutes.

Meanwhile, preheat the oven to 200° C/400° F, gas mark 6.

Fold the fillets and arrange in a baking dish. Dice 25 g/1 oz of the butter and dot it over. Season, cover with foil and bake for 7-10 minutes, or until tender.

Strain the fish stock, measure and make up to 250 ml/8 fl oz with water.

Melt 100 g/3 oz of the remaining butter, add the flour and cook, stirring, for 1 minute. Remove from the heat and stir in the fish stock and white wine. Simmer for 10 minutes, stirring occasionally. Reduce the heat and stir in the egg yolk mixture. Add 20 g/³/₄ oz butter and set aside.

Melt the remaining butter and sauté all the prawns for 3-5 minutes.

Place the sole on a serving dish, garnish with the prawns and sauce and serve.

BAKED WHITING

Serves 6

6 whiting, filleted
juice of 2 lemons
2 tbsp vegetable oil
1 tbsp chopped parsley
salt
3 tbsp breadcrumbs
50 g/2 oz butter, diced

Preheat the oven to 180° C/350° F, gas mark 4. Arrange the fillets in one layer in a large ovenproof dish. Add the lemon juice, oil and parsley and season with salt. Sprinkle over the breadcrumbs and dot with the butter. Bake for 15-20 minutes, until tender.

Serve immediately in the baking dish, accompanied by a green salad.

COD IN RED WINE

Serves 8

25 g/1 oz flour
salt and freshly ground black pepper
1 x 2 kg/4lb cod, skinned
150 ml/5 fl oz vegetable oil
100 ml/4 fl oz white wine
juice of 2 lemons
50 g/2 oz bacon, derinded and chopped
170 g/6 oz breadcrumbs
50 g/2 oz butter
200 g/7 oz new potatoes, scrubbed
100 g/4 oz mushrooms, sliced
2 tbsp mayonnaise
1 tbsp chopped parsley

Red wine sauce:
150 g/5 oz butter
1 carrot, peeled and chopped
1 onion, peeled and chopped
1 tbsp flour
100 ml/4 fl oz red wine
200 ml/7 fl oz stock
8 canned anchovies, drained
tsp cayenne pepper
100 ml/4 fl oz single cream

Preheat the oven to 200° C/400° F, gas mark 6.

Season the flour and coat the fish. Place the fish in a large, ovenproof casserole and add the oil, wine, lemon juice and bacon. Sprinkle over the breadcrumbs, and dot with half the butter. Cover and bake, basting occasionally, for 20-25 minutes.

Meanwhile, cook the potatoes in lightly

Left: Cod in Red Wine
Top right: Baked Whiting
Bottom right: Sole with Prawns

Below: Sautéed Haddock
Right: Sole with Prawns (see page 8)

salted boiling water for 15-20 minutes. Drain and reserve.

Melt the remaining butter and sauté the mushrooms for 3-5 minutes. Set aside.

Remove the casserole from the oven and add the potatoes, mushrooms and mayonnaise. Cover and set aside.

To make the sauce, melt 25 g/1 oz of the butter and cook the carrot and onion for 5-7 minutes, until soft. Add the flour and cook, stirring, for 1 minute. Remove

from the heat and stir in the wine and stock. Return to the heat and bring to the boil, stirring. Simmer, stirring until thickened. Work the mixture in a blender or food processor and return to the pan.

Mash the anchovies with 25 g/1 oz of the remaining butter and stir into the sauce. Season the remaining butter with the cayenne pepper and stir into the sauce. Finally stir in the cream over low heat.

Arrange the fish on a large serving plate and spoon over the sauce in which it was cooked. Sprinkle over the parsley. Garnish with the potatoes and mushrooms and serve the red wine sauce separately.

SAUTEED HADDOCK

Serves 6

1.25 kg/2 lb haddock fillets
25 g/1 oz flour
salt and freshly ground white pepper
100 ml/4 fl oz vegetable oil
250 g/8 oz onions, peeled and chopped
1 garlic clove, peeled and crushed
500 g/1 lb tomatoes, skinned and seeded
300 g/10 oz shelled peas
1 red pepper, seeded and cut into strips
2 hard-boiled eggs, shelled and halved

Cut the fish into bite-sized pieces and coat with flour seasoned with salt and pepper. Heat the oil and fry the fish for 5 minutes until golden. Transfer the fish to a flameproof casserole and set aside.

Sauté the onions and garlic in the same oil for 5-7 minutes. Add the tomatoes, peas and red pepper. Cook for 5 minutes, stirring occasionally.

Pour the vegetable mixture over the fish, cover and simmer for about 15 minutes, or until cooked through. If the sauce is drying out, add a little water.

Transfer the fish and sauce to a serving dish and serve, garnished with the eggs.

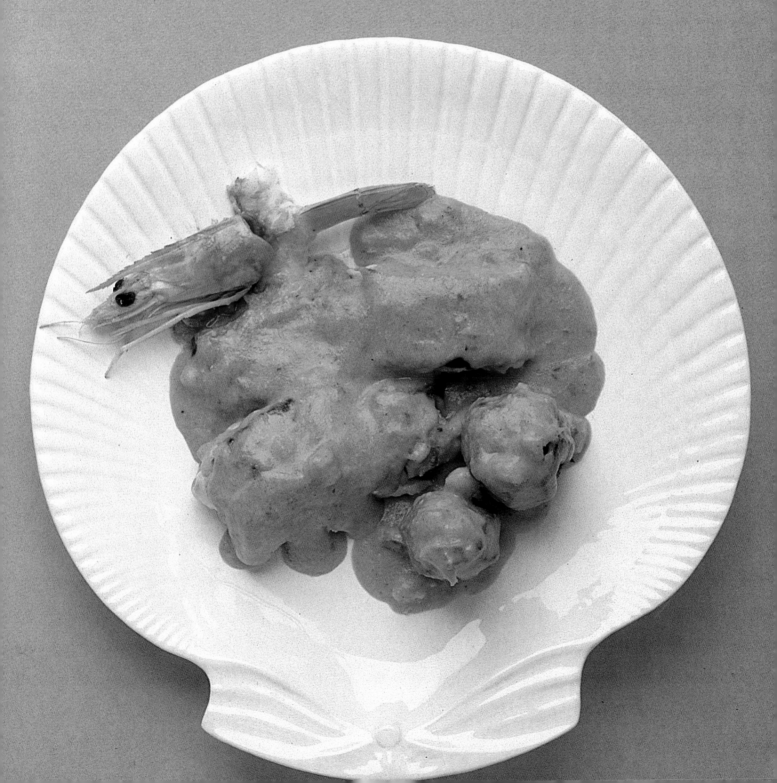

COD WITH PRAWN SAUCE

Serves 6

10 small potatoes, washed and dried
1 tbsp vegetable oil
1 x 1 kg/3 lb cod fillet
salt
25 g/1 oz flour
150 g/5 oz butter
juice of 1 lemon

Prawn sauce:
300 ml/10 fl oz milk
1 bay leaf
6 black peppercorns
1 slice onion
1 mace blade
125 g/4 oz butter
25 g/1 oz flour
250 g/8 oz prawns
250 g/8 oz Mediterranean or Pacific prawns

Preheat the oven to 190° C/375° F, gas mark 5.

Prick the potato skins, brush with a little oil and bake for 30-40 minutes.

Skin the fish, remove the bones and cut the flesh into two. Rub both sides of each piece with salt and coat with flour. Heat a metal skewer until it is very hot and press it gently across fish to make criss-cross lines.

Brush an ovenproof casserole with a little of the oil. Melt the butter. Arrange the fish in the casserole and sprinkle over the butter and lemon juice. Cover and bake for 25-30 minutes, or until tender.

To make the sauce, heat the milk, bay leaf, peppercorns, onion and mace to just below boiling point. Remove from the heat and set aside to infuse for 10 minutes. Strain the milk and discard the flavourings.

Meanwhile, peel and devein the prawns and Mediterranean prawns, reserving the shells. Chop the prawns. Mash together the prawn shells and 100 g/3 oz of the butter. Work the mixture in a blender or food mill until smooth. Stir in the chopped prawns.

Melt the remaining butter and stir in the flour. Cook, stirring, for 1 minute. Remove the pan from the heat and gradually stir in the flavoured milk. Return to the heat and bring to the boil, stirring. Cook, stirring for 1-2 minutes. Stir in the prawn butter and chopped prawn mixture.

Remove the potatoes from the oven. Cut off their tops and scoop out the flesh. Fill with a little prawn sauce and return to the oven for 5-10 minutes to brown.

Transfer the fish to a serving plate. Pour over the remaining sauce and garnish with the stuffed potatoes.

STUFFED WHITING

Serves 6

4 tbsp olive oil
1 kg/2 lb whiting in one piece
1 garlic clove, peeled and crushed
1 tbsp chopped parsley
salt
juice of 1 lemon
125 g/4 oz butter
300 g/10 oz prawns, peeled, deveined and chopped
2 hard-boiled eggs, shelled and quartered
100 g/3 oz ham, minced
2 tbsp dry sherry
100 g/4 oz breadcrumbs
500 g/1 lb spinach

Sauce:
25 g/1 oz butter
15 g/ oz flour
250 ml/8 fl oz fish stock
juice of 1 lemon
2 tbsp dry sherry

Preheat the oven to 180° C/350° F, gas mark 4. Brush a baking sheet with a little of the oil.

Slit the fish on one side and remove the bones. Mix together the garlic, parsley, salt, lemon juice and the remaining oil to make a paste and brush half the mixture over the inside of the fish. Dice 75 g/3 oz of the butter and dot half inside the fish. Stuff with half the prawns and the hard-boiled eggs. Close the fish with fine thread to keep the stuffing in place. Cover with the remaining parsley paste and sprinkle over the ham.

Arrange the fish on the prepared baking sheet and dot with the remaining diced butter. Sprinkle over the sherry and breadcrumbs and bake in the oven for 20 minutes, or until cooked.

To make the sauce, melt the butter and stir in the flour. Cook, stirring, for 1 minute. Remove the pan from the heat and gradually stir in the fish stock. Return to the heat and bring to the boil, stirring. Simmer, stirring, for 1-2 minutes. Remove from the heat and stir in the lemon juice and sherry. Keep warm.

Rinse the spinach and pat dry. Remove the stalks and shred the leaves. Melt the remaining butter in a frying-pan and sauté the spinach and remaining prawns for 1-2 minutes.

Remove the fish from the oven and transfer it to a serving dish. Remove and discard the thread. Make a border of spinach and prawns and spoon over the sauce.

NUTTY HADDOCK

Serves 6

1.25 kg/2 lb haddock
salt and freshly ground black pepper
1 tbsp flour
approximately 250 ml/8 fl oz vegetable oil
100g/3 oz blanched almonds
4 slices bread, crusts removed
3 garlic cloves, peeled and crushed
1 tbsp chopped parsley
1 bay leaf

Cut the fish in pieces. Season and coat in flour. Heat half the oil and fry the fish pieces until lightly golden. Transfer them to a flameproof casserole.

Fry the almonds and bread in the same oil, adding more oil if required. Drain on absorbent paper and allow to cool. Pound in a mortar with 2 garlic cloves and the parsley. Add the mixture to the fish with the remaining oil, the remaining garlic and the bay leaf. Adjust the seasoning.

Cover and cook over gentle heat for 10-15 minutes, or until the sauce thickens and the fish is cooked through. Serve at once.

SPARKLING SOLE

Serves 3

3 sole, filleted
100 g/3 oz butter
200 ml/7 fl oz sparkling wine
salt and freshly ground black pepper
3 egg yolks
100 ml/4 fl oz single cream

Garnish:
50 g/2 oz butter
3 bananas, peeled and sliced
pinch cayenne pepper

Arrange the sole fillets, without folding, in a large pan. Add 25 g/1 oz of the butter, the wine and seasoning. Poach for 7-8 minutes. Allow to cool in the liquid.

To make the garnish, melt the butter, add the banana slices and sprinkle over the cayenne pepper. Toss the slices gently until glazed. Set aside.

Transfer the fish to a large serving dish and reserve the cooking liquid.

Melt the remaining butter. Beat the egg yolks with 3 tbsp of the fish cooking liquid. Beat in the melted butter, the cream and the remaining cooking liquid.

Pour the sauce over the fish, garnish with the banana slices and serve.

Top: Nutty Haddock
Bottom: Sparkling Sole

SAFFRON COD

Serves 6

1 tbsp vegetable oil
2 garlic cloves, peeled
200 g/3 oz flour
salt and freshly ground black pepper
1 kg/2 lb cod steaks
100 ml/4 fl oz white wine
500 ml/17 fl oz fish or chicken stock
1/2 tsp saffron threads
1 tbsp water
1 tbsp chopped parsley

Heat the oil and sauté the whole garlic cloves for 5 minutes, or until golden. Transfer them to a mortar.

Season the flour and coat the fish. Fry the fish in the same oil for 2 minutes on each side, or until golden. Add the wine and 125 ml/4 fl oz of the stock. Cook for 2-3 minutes.

Meanwhile, add a little salt, the saffron and the water to the garlic and pound with a pestle until smooth. Pour over the fish and add as much of the remaining stock as necessary to prevent the fish drying out.

Add the parsley and cook for 10 minutes, or until cooked. Serve hot.

WHITING IN CHEESE SAUCE

Serves 4

400 g/14 oz potatoes, peeled
600 g/1 lb whiting fillets
75 g/3 oz butter
100 ml/4 fl oz white wine
juice of 1 lemon
salt and freshly ground black pepper
500 ml/17 fl oz milk
50 g/2 oz flour
1 egg yolk
4 tbsp tomato purée
50 g/2 oz grated Cheddar cheese

Preheat the oven to 180° C/350° F, gas mark 4.

Cut the potatoes into small pieces and cook in lightly salted boiling water for 20 minutes, or until tender.

Place the fish in an ovenproof casserole. Dot with 25 g/1 oz of the butter and pour over the wine and lemon juice. Season, cover and bake for 10 minutes.

Transfer the fish to a flameproof dish. Reserve the cooking liquid. Preheat the grill.

Drain and mash the potatoes with 25 g/

1 oz butter, 2 tbsp milk and the egg yolk. Season well. Make a border of mashed potato around the fish.

Melt the remaining butter and stir in the flour. Cook, stirring, for 1 minute. Remove from the heat and gradually stir in the remaining milk. Return to the heat and bring to the boil, stirring. Simmer for 1-2 minutes, stirring. Stir in the reserved cooking liquid and the tomato purée.

Pour the sauce over the fish and sprinkle over the cheese. Grill for 5 minutes until warmed through, golden and bubbling.

SOLE ESPERANZA

Serves 4

500 g/1 lb hake fillets
1 egg white
salt and freshly ground white pepper
250 ml/8 fl oz single cream
2 large sole, filleted
juice of 1 lemon
white wine
25 g/1 oz butter, melted
2 hard-boiled eggs, shelled and sliced

Top left: Saffron Cod
Bottom Left: Whiting in Cheese Sauce
Right: Sole Esperanza

black and green olives, stoned and sliced
1 tomato, thinly sliced
lettuce

Esperanza sauce:
500 g/1 lb spinach
2 egg yolks
250 ml/8 fl oz vegetable oil
salt and freshly ground black pepper

Finely chop the hake fillets. Stir in the egg white and seasoning. Beat in the cream, a little at a time.

Spread out the sole fillets and season with salt and pepper. Divide the stuffing equally between them and roll up tightly. Place in a dish, seam side down, and sprinkle over the lemon juice, wine and butter. Cover with greaseproof paper and set aside to chill.

To make the sauce, trim the spinach stalks and wash the leaves in cold water. Cook in the water clinging to the leaves for 5-6 minutes. Drain and press out excess water. Roughly chop the leaves.

Beat the egg yolks, then beat in the oil, a few drops at a time. When all the oil has been absorbed, add the spinach and work the mixture in a blender until smooth. Season.

Remove the fish from the refrigerator and cut into slices. Arrange on a serving plate and garnish with the eggs, olives, tomatoes, lettuce and a little sauce. Serve the remaining sauce separately.

FISH GOUJONS

Serves 4

800 g/2 lb plaice fillets
juice of ½ lemon
salt and freshly ground black pepper
25 g/1 oz flour
1 egg, lightly beaten
125 g/4 oz breadcrumbs
oil for deep-frying
1 lemon, thinly sliced

Cut the fish into thin strips. Sprinkle over the lemon juice and season. Coat with flour, beaten egg and breadcrumbs. Roll the strips gently between the palms of your hands.

Heat the oil to 190° C/375° F, or until a cube of stale bread turns golden in 30 seconds.

Fry the goujons for 5-7 minutes until golden. Drain on absorbent paper. Arrange on a serving dish and garnish with the lemon slices.

PLAICE WITH CLAMS

Serves 6

3 plaice, filleted, trimmings reserved
425 ml/15 fl oz water
200 ml/7 fl oz white wine
150 g/5 oz butter
12 clams
1 tsp cornflour
4 egg yolks
100 ml/4 fl oz single cream

Make a stock by simmering the fish trimmings, skin, water, white wine and 50 g/2 oz of the butter for 30 minutes. Strain the stock.

Arrange the plaice in a large pan. Pour over the stock and poach for 6-7 minutes. Leave to cool in the stock, then transfer the fish to a flameproof dish.

Scrub the clams under cold running water. Discard any that do not shut when sharply tapped. Put the clams in the stock and bring to the boil. Continue boiling until the shells open. Drain. Strain the stock through clean muslin. Reserve 3 tbsp of the stock and boil the remainder until it has reduced slightly.

Mix 1 tbsp of the boiling stock with the cornflour and then stir the mixture into the pan of stock. Cook, stirring, until thickened. Strain, measure 500 ml/17 fl oz and set aside.

Preheat the grill. Melt the remaining butter. Beat the egg yolks with the 3 tbsp of reserved stock in a heatproof bowl over hot water. Beat the thickened stock into the egg yolk mixture. Stir in the cream.

Arrange the clams on top of the fish and pour over the sauce. Place under the grill for 5-8 minutes, until very hot and serve immediately.

Left: Fish Goujons
Below: Plaice with Clams

HALIBUT IN PRAWN AND BRANDY SAUCE

Serves 6

1 kg/2 lb halibut
50 g/2 oz butter
juice of 1 lemon
salt and freshly ground black pepper

Sauce:
250 g/8 oz prawns
50 g/2 oz butter
1 tsp flour
1 small onion, peeled and chopped
2 tbsp brandy
2 tbsp tomato purée
200 ml/7 fl oz fish stock

Preheat the oven to 190° C/375° F, gas mark 5.

Remove the bones from the fish and cut into three large pieces. Grease an ovenproof casserole with a little of the butter and arrange the fish in it. Dot the remaining butter on top, add the lemon juice and season. Cover and bake for 20-30 minutes, or until tender.

Meanwhile, make the sauce. Peel the prawns, reserving the trimmings. Soften half the butter with a fork and incorporate the flour to make *beurre manié* and set aside. Melt the remaining butter and fry the onion for 7-8 minutes until golden. Add the prawn heads and shells and pound the mixture in a mortar or work in a food processor until smooth. Return to the pan and add the brandy. Heat gently and then ignite, shaking the pan gently until the flames die down. Stir in the tomato purée and stock, bring to the boil and simmer for 10 minutes.

Strain the sauce and gradually beat in the *beurre manié*, a little at a time, over low heat, beating well to incorporate fully before adding the next piece. When it has all been incorporated, add the prawns and cook for 2-3 minutes, until heated through.

Transfer the fish to a serving dish. Pour over the sauce and serve immediately.

FISH IN MUSTARD SAUCE

Serves 6

100 g/3 oz butter
1 onion, peeled and grated
50 g/2 oz flour
500 ml/17 fl oz warm milk
100 ml/4 fl oz cream
1 tbsp mustard
salt and freshly ground black pepper
1 kg/3 lb white fish fillets

Melt the butter over very low heat and cook the onion slowly to make a purée. Stir in the flour and cook, stirring, for 1 minute. Gradually stir in the warm milk and seasoning and bring to the boil, stirring. Simmer, stirring, for 1-2 minutes.

Stir in the cream and the mustard. Taste and, if necessary, adjust the seasoning.

Add the fish and cook for 8-10 minutes, or until tender.

Transfer to a serving dish and serve immediately, accompanied by potatoes parboiled and sautéed in butter.

Top left: Hake with Fried Vegetable Sauce
Bottom left: Fish in Mustard Sauce

HAKE WITH FRIED VEGETABLE SAUCE

Serves 6

1.5 kg/3 lb hake fillets
50 g/2 oz butter
juice of 1 lemon
salt and freshly ground black pepper
50 ml/2 fl oz vegetable oil
3 onions, peeled and chopped
2 courgettes, trimmed and sliced
12 tomatoes, skinned, seeded and chopped
225 ml/8 fl oz brandy
1 kg/2 lb potatoes, boiled and mashed

Preheat the oven to 190° C/375° F, gas mark 5.

Arrange the fish in an ovenproof casserole, dot with half the butter, sprinkle over the lemon juice and season. Bake for 12-15 minutes, or until tender.

Melt the remaining butter with the oil and fry the onion for 5 minutes, or until soft. Add the courgettes and tomatoes and cook over low heat, stirring occasionally, for 10 minutes.

Work the mixture in a food processor or blender, or put it through a mincer. Return to the pan and add the brandy. Season with pepper and cook for 10 minutes.

Place the potatoes on a large serving dish and arrange the fish on top. Spoon over the fried vegetable sauce. Serve with Hollandaise sauce, if liked (see page 34).

COD PIL-PIL

Serves 6

1 kg/2 lb salt cod
300 ml/ 10 fl oz vegetable oil
1 garlic bulb, peeled and thinly sliced

Soak the cod in cold water for 12 hours or overnight, changing the water several times. Drain and set aside.

Heat the oil in a flameproof, earthenware dish★ and fry the garlic for 6-8 minutes. Remove the dish from the heat.

Remove the garlic and arrange the cod, skin side downwards, in the dish. Return to very low heat and cook gently and slowly for 1 hour, shaking the dish from time to time. If necessary, place the dish slightly to the side of the hob to ensure very slow cooking.

Return the dish to the hob and increase the heat. Return the garlic to the dish. Twirl the dish vigorously and continuously over the heat until the sauce is bubbling (making a 'pil-pil' sound). If the sauce does not make this sound, add 1 tsp cold water to the edge of the dish, taking care not to burn yourself.

Serve immediately.

★ Note
This traditional Spanish dish is best cooked in a round earthenware *cazuela*.

RED BREAM IN CHILI SAUCE

Serves 6

1 large red bream
50 g/2 oz flour
140 ml/5 fl oz vegetable oil
4 chili peppers, seeded and sliced
3 garlic cloves, peeled and crushed
12 blanched almonds
2 slices bread, crusts removed
100 ml/4 fl oz tomato purée

Remove the bones, cut the bream into chunks and coat with half the flour. Heat 25 ml/1 fl oz of the oil in a frying-pan and fry the fish for 5-6 minutes until golden. Remove the fish from the pan with a slotted spoon and set aside in a flameproof casserole.

Fry the chili peppers, garlic, almonds and bread in the same oil. Remove with a slotted spoon and pound in a mortar with sufficient water to form a purée. Alternatively, work the mixture in a blender or food processor.

Heat the remaining oil and stir in the remaining flour, the tomato purée and the chili mixture. Add more water if the sauce is too thick. Pour the sauce over the bream and cook for 10 minutes, or until tender.

Serve immediately.

Below: Cod pil-pil

BAKED TURBOT

Serves 6

50 ml/2 fl oz vegetable oil
4 potatoes, peeled and thinly sliced
1 kg/2 lb turbot steaks
1 tbsp butter
250 g/8 oz small onions, peeled
1 tbsp sugar
500 ml/17 fl oz chicken stock
200 ml/7 fl oz cream

Preheat the oven to 160° C/325° F, gas mark 3.

Put half the oil in an ovenproof casserole and arrange the potato slices on the bottom of the dish. Place the turbot steaks on top and sprinkle over the remaining oil. Cover and bake for 20 minutes, or until the fish is tender. Do not allow it to overcook.

Meanwhile, glaze the onions. Melt the butter in a frying-pan, add the onions and the sugar and cook over high heat, stirring occasionally, until they are golden. Pour over half the stock and bring to the boil. Transfer the mixture to an ovenproof dish and continue cooking in the oven for 15 minutes, or until tender.

Transfer the turbot to a large serving dish. Arrange the potato slices on one side of the dish and the glazed onions on the other. Keep warm while you make the sauce.

To make the sauce, mix together the remaining stock and the turbot cooking juices. Bring to the boil and allow to reduce by half. Stir in the cream. Spoon a little of the sauce over the fish and serve the remainder separately in a sauceboat.

HAKE IN SHERRY SAUCE

Serves 4

125 g/4 oz butter
800 g/1 lb hake fillets
salt
3 tbsp breadcrumbs
yolks of 2 hard-boiled eggs, crumbled
250 ml/8 fl oz sherry

Preheat the oven to 190° C/375° F, gas mark 5.

Grease a baking dish with a little of the butter and arrange the hake fillets in two rows side by side. Dice all but 25 g/1 oz of the remaining butter and dot over the fish. Sprinkle with salt and bake for 15-20 minutes, or until tender.

Transfer the fish to a serving dish and keep warm while you make the sauce. Reserve the cooking juices.

Melt the remaining butter in a frying-pan. Stir in the breadcrumbs and crumbled egg yolks. Add the sherry and the reserved cooking juices. If the sauce is too thick, dilute it with a little water or fish stock.

When it is hot, spoon the sauce over the fish. Serve immediately, accompanied by fried diced potatoes.

HAKE WITH ANCHOVIES AND CAPERS

Serves 6

6 hake steaks
salt and freshly ground black pepper
juice of 1 lemon
100 ml/4 fl oz vegetable oil
100 ml/4 fl oz white wine

Garnish:
6 lemon slices
40 g/1 oz butter
100 g/3 oz canned anchovies, drained
75 g/2 oz capers
25 g/1 oz black olives, stoned and halved
25 g/1 oz green olives, stoned and halved
1 tbsp chopped parsley

Preheat the oven to 190° C/375° F, gas mark 5.

Season the steaks well and sprinkle over the lemon juice, oil and white wine. Bake for about 15 minutes, or until tender.

Arrange the fish on a large serving dish and put a slice of lemon and knob of butter on each one. Garnish with rolled anchovies, capers, olives and parsley.

Serve with rice and mayonnaise or Hollandaise sauce (see page 34).

SWORDFISH WITH CLAMS

Serves 6

1 kg/2 lb swordfish fillets
salt and freshly ground black pepper
50 g/2 oz flour
50 ml/2 fl oz vegetable oil
500 g/1 lb clams
1 onion, peeled and finely chopped
2 garlic cloves, peeled and crushed
100 ml/4 fl oz white wine
1/2 tsp saffron threads

Coat the fish in seasoned flour. Heat half the oil and fry the fish for 5-6 minutes, until golden but not cooked through. Transfer the fish to a flameproof casserole and set aside.

Scrub the clams under cold running water and discard any that do not shut immediately when sharply tapped. Put them in a pan, cover with water and bring to the boil. Boil until the shells have opened. Drain and reserve the cooking liquid. Discard any clams that have not opened. Remove the clams from their shells and place them in the casserole with the fish. Strain the cooking liquid through a cloth to remove any grit and reserve.

Add the rest of the oil to the frying-pan and cook the onion and garlic for 5 minutes, until soft. Add the wine and reserved cooking liquid and bring to the boil. Allow to reduce slightly.

Pound the saffron with a little salt in a mortar, then stir into the sauce. Pour the sauce over the fish and cook on a low heat, shaking the pan from time to time, for 10 minutes, or until the fish is cooked through and very hot. Serve immediately.

HAKE WITH ASPARAGUS

Serves 6

1 tbsp vegetable oil
1 bunch asparagus, trimmed and peeled
salt
1.5 kg/3 lb hake
2 eggs, lightly beaten
100 g/3 oz breadcrumbs
75 g/3 oz butter
140 ml/5 fl oz sherry
1 large onion, peeled and finely chopped
6 carrots, peeled and finely diced

Preheat the oven to 190° C/375° F, gas mark 5. Brush a baking tin with the oil.

Tie the asparagus in a bundle and cook, upright and covered, in boiling salted water for 25-30 minutes, or until tender. Alternatively, cook in a steamer.

Cut the hake in half and remove the bones. Rub the skin side with salt. Brush the tops of the hake pieces with the beaten egg, sprinkle over the breadcrumbs and press in place with your fingers. Dice 25 g/1 oz of the butter and dot over the fish. Sprinkle over 1 tbsp of the sherry and bake for about 20 minutes, or until tender.

Melt the remaining butter and sauté the onion and carrot for 7-10 minutes, or until cooked. Season, remove from the heat and stir in the remaining sherry.

Drain the asparagus on a clean tea towel on a plate and untie.

Arrange the hake on a serving dish and garnish with the carrot and onion mixture. Serve immediately with the asparagus.

Top: Hake with Anchovies and Capers
Bottom: Hake with Asparagus

SPANISH CONGER EEL

Serves 4

100 g/4 oz butter
100 ml/4 fl oz vegetable oil
4 conger eel steaks
150 g/5 oz small onions, peeled
100 ml/4 fl oz white wine
1 tbsp chopped parsley
salt and freshly ground white pepper
1 tsp flour
4 parsley sprigs

Melt 50 g/2 oz of the butter with the oil and fry the eel and the onions for 5–8 minutes, or until lightly browned on both sides. Add the wine and parsley and season with salt and pepper. Cover and cook over low heat, shaking the pan from time to time, for 40 minutes, or until tender.

Arrange the fish and onions on a serving dish. Reserve the cooking liquid.

Melt the remaining butter and stir in the flour. Remove the pan from the heat and gradually stir in the reserved cooking liquid. Return to the heat and bring to the boil, stirring. Simmer, stirring, for 1–2 minutes. If the sauce is too thick, stir in a little milk. Pour the sauce over the fish, garnish with the parsley sprigs and serve immediately with Lyonnaise potatoes and grilled tomatoes.

JOHN DORY FLORENTINE

Serves 6

1 kg/2 lb spinach
100 g/3 oz butter
40 g/1 oz flour
250 ml/8 fl oz fish stock
250 ml/8 fl oz milk
salt and freshly ground black pepper
100 ml/4 fl oz cream
12 John Dory fillets★
1 tbsp grated cheese

Preheat the oven to 190° C/375° F, gas mark 5.

Trim the stalks and wash the spinach. Cook with only the water clinging to the leaves for about 7 minutes, or until just tender. Drain, press out any excess water and finely chop the leaves. Melt half the butter in a frying-pan and sauté the spinach for 2–3 minutes. Arrange the spinach to cover the bottom of an ovenproof dish and set aside.

Melt the remaining butter and stir in the flour. Cook, stirring, for 1 minute. Remove from the heat and gradually stir in the fish stock and the milk. Return the pan to the heat and bring to the boil, stirring. Simmer, stirring for 1–2 minutes. Season and stir in the cream. Set aside. Season the fish and fold the fillets in half with the skin on the inside. Arrange them on top of the spinach and pour over the white sauce. Sprinkle over the cheese and bake for about 20 minutes, or until cooked through.

Serve immediately.

★ Note: Ask the fishmonger for the trimmings for making the fish stock.

Left: Spanish Conger Eel
Below: John Dory Florentine

HAKE AND TOMATO SAUCE

Serves 6

100 g/3 oz butter
1 large onion, peeled and chopped
500 g/1 lb tomatoes, skinned and chopped
1 kg/2 lb hake fillets
salt and freshly ground black pepper
100 ml/4 fl oz white wine
1 tbsp chopped parsley

Melt 50 g/1 oz of the butter and fry the onion for 5 minutes. Add the tomatoes and cook over low heat for 10 minutes.

Put the hake in a large pan, season, pour over the wine and poach for 6-8 minutes.

Transfer the hake to a serving dish. Stir the cooking liquid into the tomato sauce, add the remaining butter and stir until it has melted. Pour the sauce over the fish.

Garnish with the parsley and serve.

BAKED SEA BREAM

Serves 6

1 large sea bream, cleaned and scaled
1 lemon, thinly sliced
6 parsley sprigs
salt
200 ml/7 fl oz vegetable oil
4 garlic cloves, peeled and crushed
1 dried chili pepper, chopped
100 g/3 oz breadcrumbs
1 tbsp white wine vinegar
3 lemon slices

Preheat the oven to 200° C/400° F, gas mark 6. Make crosswise cuts along the length of the fish and insert a lemon slice and parsley sprig in each. Season with salt. Place the fish in a baking tin and set aside.

Heat the oil and fry the chili pepper and garlic for 3-5 minutes. Pour over the fish, sprinkle over the breadcrumbs and bake for 20-30 minutes, or until tender.

Transfer the fish to a large serving dish. Pour the cooking liquid into a pan, stir in the vinegar and heat gently. Spoon a little sauce over the fish, garnish with lemon slices and serve with fried bread triangles.

MARINATED RED MULLET

Serves 4

140 ml/5 fl oz olive oil
juice of 2 lemons
300 g/ 10 oz onions, peeled and chopped
1 tbsp chopped parsley
salt and freshly ground black pepper
4 red mullet, cleaned and bones removed

200 g/7 oz canned anchovies, drained
75 g/2 oz butter
1 tbsp flour

Garnish:
20 canned anchovy fillets, drained
1 lemon, sliced
black olives
parsley sprigs

Make a marinade by mixing together the oil, lemon juice, onions, parsley and seasoning. Pour over the fish and place in the refrigerator for at least 2 hours.

Preheat the oven to 200° C/400° F, gas mark 6. Mash the anchovies and butter together. Divide into four portions and place one inside each drained fish. Close the cavities with cocktail sticks. Arrange in a baking dish, sprinkle over the flour and bake for 10 minutes, or until tender.

To garnish, arrange the anchovies on the mullet and return to the oven for 2-3 minutes. Transfer to a serving plate, remove the cocktail sticks and garnish.

Top left: Hake and Tomato Sauce
Bottom left: Baked Sea Bream
Below: Red Mullet Parcels
Bottom: Marinated Red Mullet

RED MULLET PARCELS

Serves 6

6 red mullet, cleaned and scaled
salt and freshly ground black pepper
75 g/3 oz butter
2 leeks, trimmed and finely chopped
1 celery stalk, trimmed and chopped
100 ml/4 fl oz bianco vermouth
juice of 2 lemons
100 ml/4 fl oz fish stock

Wash the fish, pat dry, season with salt and pepper and set aside.

Melt 50 g/2 oz of the butter and sauté the leeks for 3-5 minutes. Add the celery, cover and cook for 8-10 minutes. Stir in the vermouth and lemon juice, bring to the boil and allow to reduce slightly. Stir in the fish stock and cook for 5 minutes.

Grease six squares of aluminium foil with the remaining butter. Put one fish on each square and spoon over the vegetable mixture. Fold over the sides of the foil and seal the edges. Set aside for 1 hour.

Preheat the oven to 200° C/400° F, gas mark 6. Arrange the parcels on a baking sheet and cook for 14 minutes, or until cooked through. Serve in the parcels.

QUICK AND EASY HAKE

Serves 6

1 kg/2 lb hake steaks
salt and freshly ground black pepper
25 g/1 oz flour
100 ml 4 fl oz vegetable oil
2 garlic cloves, peeled and finely chopped
2 tbsp chopped parsley
juice of 2 lemons

Season the hake and coat with the flour. Heat the oil and cook the fish until golden on both sides. Remove and keep warm. Drain off half the oil and heat the remainder. Fry the garlic and parsley for 3-5 minutes. Stir in the lemon juice and cook for 2-3 minutes. Return the fish to the pan and serve with chips.

BRAISED SEA BREAM

Serves 6

1 kg/2 lb sea bream
salt and freshly ground black pepper
100 ml/4 fl oz vegetable oil
2 potatoes, peeled and thinly sliced
3 garlic cloves, peeled and finely chopped
1 tbsp chopped parsley
50 ml/2 fl oz white wine vinegar

Preheat the oven to 200° C/400° F, gas mark 6.

Clean and scale the fish. Cut it into fillets or slices, wash and pat dry. Season with salt and pepper.

Heat half the oil in a frying-pan and fry the potato slices until they are beginning to turn gold. Remove with a slotted spoon and transfer to an ovenproof casserole. Arrange the fish on top and sprinkle over the garlic, parsley, remaining oil and vinegar.

Bake in the oven, shaking the casserole dish from time to time and basting with the cooking juices, for 20-25 minutes, or until tender.

Serve immediately.

CRISPY COD BALLS

Serves 6

500 g/1 lb salt cod fillet
oil for deep-frying

Batter:
100 g/4 oz flour
salt
1 tbsp vegetable oil
150 ml/5 fl oz tepid water
2 egg whites, stiffly whisked

Soak the cod overnight in cold water, changing the water from time. Drain.

Put the cod in a pan, pour over cold water to cover and poach for 10 minutes. Drain and flake the fish.

To make the batter, sift the flour and a pinch of salt into a bowl. Stir in the oil and enough water to make a smooth batter that will coat the back of the spoon. Fold the egg whites into the batter.

Heat the oil to 190° C/375° or until a cube of stale bread turns golden in 30 seconds.

Shape the cod into balls with two teaspoons. Dip the balls in the batter and deep-fry in batches until puffy and golden. Drain on absorbent paper.

ROAST SEA BREAM

Serves 6

1 large sea bream
salt
1 lemon, sliced
1 garlic clove, peeled and thinly sliced
150 ml/5 fl oz vegetable oil
1 tsp paprika
225 ml/8 fl oz white wine
50 g/2 oz mixed nuts, ground
juice of 1 lemon

Preheat the oven to 200° C/400° F, gas mark 6.

Clean the fish and season inside and out with salt. Peel and halve 2 or 3 slices of lemon, reserving the remainder. Make four or five slits along one side of the fish and insert half a lemon slice and a sliver of garlic in each.

Brush a baking tin with a little of the oil. Mix the remaining oil with paprika to taste. Place the fish in the baking tin and pour over the flavoured oil. Bake for 10 minutes.

Add the wine and cook for a further 20 minutes, basting the fish from time to time.

Remove the fish from the oven and transfer to a serving dish. Mix the nuts with the lemon juice and stir into the cooking juices. Heat the mixture, shaking the pan gently from time to time, until thickened.

Pour the sauce over the fish, garnish with the remaining lemon slices and serve.

HAKE IN GREEN SAUCE

Serves 6

1 kg/2 lb hake steaks
salt and freshly ground black pepper
25 g/1 oz flour
3 garlic cloves, peeled and crushed
200 ml/7 fl oz vegetable oil
2 tbsp chopped parsley
18 clams
250 g/8 oz cooked peas

Season the hake steaks with salt and pepper and coat with flour. Heat the oil in a frying-pan, add the garlic and fish and sprinkle over the parsley. Cook, shaking the pan from time to time, until the hake loses its transparency and becomes opaque white.

Meanwhile, scrub the clams under cold running water, discarding any that do not shut immediately when sharply tapped.

Add the peas and the clams to the pan and cook, shaking the pan from time to time, until the shellfish open. Discard any that remain shut.

Remove the pan from the heat and continue shaking it until the sauce jellifies. Transfer to a serving dish and serve immediately.

Right above: Hake in Green Sauce
Right below: Braised Sea Bream

CHAMPAGNE TURBOT

Serves 6

1 small turbot, cleaned
salt and freshly ground black pepper
140 g/5 oz butter
1 garlic clove, peeled and thinly sliced
4 leeks, trimmed and cut into matchstick strips
1/2 bottle Champagne or sparkling white wine
300 ml/10 fl oz fish stock
25 g/1 oz flour
200 ml/7 fl oz double cream
250 g/ 8 oz mushrooms, thinly sliced
1 large truffle, sliced

Preheat the oven to 160° C/325° F, gas mark 3.

Cut through the black side of the turbot and detach the fillets. Season and place in a baking tin. Dot with 75 g/3 oz of the butter and sprinkle over the garlic and leeks. Pour over the wine and half the stock. Bake in the oven, basting with the cooking juices from time to time, for 40 minutes, or until tender.

When the turbot is cooked, transfer it to a large serving dish. Bring the cooking liquid to the boil, allow to reduce slightly, strain and reserve.

Melt 25 g/1 oz of the remaining butter and stir in the flour. Cook, stirring, for 1 minute. Remove the pan from the heat and stir in the reserved fish stock. Return to the heat and bring to the boil, stirring. Simmer, stirring, for 1-2 minutes, or until thick and smooth. Stir in the cream, the remaining butter, the mushrooms and truffle. Cook for 2-3 minutes.

Pour the sauce over the fish and serve immediately.

BRAISED TURBOT

Serves 6

1 x 1 kg/2 lb turbot, cleaned
salt and freshly ground black pepper
1/2 bottle white wine
juice of 1 lemon
110 g/4 oz butter
1 shallot, peeled and chopped
1 tsp cornflour
4 egg yolks
100 ml/4 fl oz tomato purée

Preheat the oven to 160° C/325° F, gas mark 3.

Place the fish in a baking tin, season and pour over the wine and lemon juice. Cover with a sheet of greaseproof paper,

Left: Braised Turbot
Right: Champagne Turbot

lightly greased with a little of the butter. Bake in the oven, basting two or three times during cooking, for 30-40 minutes, or until tender.

Remove the tin from the oven and drain off and reserve almost the cooking juices. Leave a little to keep the turbot moist while you make the sauce. Cover the turbot with the greaseproof paper.

Add the shallot to the reserved cooking juices and bring to the boil. Allow to reduce slightly. Strain and blend in the cornflour. Beat in the egg yolks and the remaining butter. Return to low heat. Do not allow the sauce to boil or the eggs will curdle. Stir in the tomato purée.

Transfer the turbot to a large serving dish. Remove the skin and the bones from the sides. Pour over the sauce and serve immediately.

SALT COD BISCAY-STYLE

Serves 4

750 g/1 lb salt cod, cut in chunks
12 chili peppers
100 ml/4 fl oz vegetable oil
2 Spanish onions, peeled and chopped
1 beef tomato, skinned and chopped

Soak the cod overnight in cold water, changing the water three or four times. Soak the chilis in cold water overnight.

Drain and rinse the cod. Drain skin and seed the peppers. Mince them or work in a food processor. Set aside.

Heat the oil and sauté the onion for 5-7 minutes. Add the tomato and the chili peppers and cook for 5 minutes. Work the mixture in a blender or food processor.

Scale the cod and remove the bones. Cut into medium-sized pieces. Place in a pan, cover with tepid water and heat. When the water is just about to boil, remove from the heat and strain. Arrange the fish, skin side up, in a flameproof casserole and pour over the sauce. Set over medium heat, moving it constantly. Serve hot.

HAKE FRITTERS

Serves 6

10 frozen hake fillets, thawed
salt and freshly ground black pepper
juice of 1 lemon
oil for deep-frying

Fritter batter:
250 g/8 oz flour
1/2 tsp salt
1 tsp dried yeast
225 ml/8 fl oz tepid milk
2 eggs, lightly beaten
1 tbsp chopped parsley

Cut the fish into three pieces. Put them in a non-metal dish, season and pour over the lemon juice. Set aside to marinate.

To make the batter, sift the flour and salt into a mixing bowl and stir in the yeast. Beat in the milk and eggs and continue beating until the batter is smooth. Stir in the parsley and set aside for about 12 minutes for the yeast to take effect.

Heat the oil to 190° C/375° F or until a cube of stale bread turns golden in 30 seconds.

Remove the fish from the marinade, dip in the batter and fry in batches for 8-10 minutes, or until puffed up and golden. Drain on absorbent paper. Transfer to a serving dish and serve with tomato sauce.

HAKE IN CIDER

Serves 4

salt and freshly ground black pepper
4 x 150 g/5 oz hake steaks
25 g/1 oz flour
50 ml/2 fl oz vegetable oil
1 medium onion, peeled and chopped
1 garlic clove, peeled and crushed
125 g/4 oz ham, cut into strips
8 prawns, peeled and deveined
300 ml/10 fl oz cider
1 tbsp chopped parsley

Left: Salt Cod Biscay-style
Top right: Hake Fritters
Bottom right: Hake in Cider

Left: Hake with Tartare Sauce
Right: Stuffed Hake

Season the hake and coat with flour. Heat the oil and cook the fish on both sides until golden. Remove from the pan.

Sauté the onion for 5-7 minutes. Add the garlic, ham, seasoning, prawns, cider and parsley. Return the fish to the pan, cover and cook over low heat for 10-12 minutes, or until the fish is tender and the sauce has thickened. Serve immediately.

STUFFED HAKE

Serves 6-8

50 g/2 oz butter
2.5 kg/5 lb hake
250 g/8 oz prawns, peeled and deveined
salt and freshly ground black pepper
200 ml/7 fl oz white wine
250 ml/8 fl oz fish stock
breadcrumbs, fried in a little butter
2 tsp cornflour
200 ml/7 fl oz single cream

Garnish
12 prawns, grilled

Preheat the oven to 180° C/350° F, gas mark 4. Grease an ovenproof casserole with the butter.

Remove the backbones and skin from the hake. Reserve the largest piece and chop the remainder. Mix together the chopped hake and 100 g/3 oz of the prawns and season. Set aside.

Place the single piece of hake on a work surface. Cover with the stuffing, fold in half and secure with cocktail sticks. Place in the prepared casserole, pour over the wine and the stock, cover and bake for about 25 minutes, or until tender.

Transfer the hake to a heatproof dish, coat with the breadcrumbs and return to the oven while you make the sauce.

Strain the cooking juices into a pan and bring to the boil. Allow to reduce slightly. Mix a little of the hot stock with the cornflour and then stir it into the pan of stock. Boil, stirring, for 1–2 minutes, or until thickened and smooth. Add the remaining prawns and stir in the cream.

Transfer the hake to a serving dish, discard the cocktail sticks and spoon over a little sauce. Garnish with the prawns and serve. Serve the sauce separately.

HAKE AND TARTARE SAUCE

Serves 4

50 g/2 oz sliced bread, crusts removed
50 ml/2 fl oz milk
250 g/8 oz prawns, peeled and deveined
2 large pieces of hake taken from the centre
100 g/3 oz smoked ham, minced
3 hard-boiled eggs, shelled and finely chopped
salt
300 ml/10 fl oz fish stock

Tartare sauce:
250 ml/8 fl oz mayonnaise
2 hard-boiled egg yolks, finely chopped
5 gherkins, finely chopped
25 g/1 oz capers, finely chopped
1 tsp made mustard
salt and freshly ground white pepper

Garnish:
2 hard-boiled eggs, shelled and sliced
25 g/1 oz stoned black olives
25 g/1 oz stuffed green olives
100 g/4 oz prawns, peeled and deveined
1 can asparagus, drained

Soak the bread in the milk for 10 minutes. Mince the prawns.

Remove the backbones from the hake. Hold each fish open and fill with these layers: soaked bread, prawns, ham and hard-boiled egg. Season with salt. Secure the openings with cocktail sticks. Transfer the stuffed hake to a fish kettle and pour over the stock. Poach over low heat for 10–12 minutes, or until tender.

Remove the hake from the fish kettle and set aside to cool.

To make the tartare sauce, thoroughly mix together the mayonnaise, egg yolks, gherkins and capers. Stir in mustard and seasoning to taste.

Transfer the hake to a serving dish, add a little tartare sauce and garnish as liked. Serve the sauce separately.

BAKED SEA-BASS WITH HOLLANDAISE SAUCE

Serves 6

1 x 1 kg/2 lb sea-bass
salt and freshly ground white pepper
juice of 1 lemon
50 g/2 oz butter, melted
250 ml/8 fl oz white wine

Hollandaise sauce:
100 ml/4 fl oz white wine vinegar
1 sprig tarragon
3 egg yolks, lightly beaten
75 g/3 oz butter, melted

Preheat the oven to 180° C/350° F, gas mark 4.

Scale the fish and remove the backbone without detaching the head. Wash and pat dry. Season inside with salt, pepper and lemon juice.

Close the fish and place in a large ovenproof casserole. Pour over the melted butter and the wine. Bake, basting with the juices from time to time, for 30 minutes, or until the fish is tender.

Meanwhile, make the sauce. Heat the vinegar and tarragon to just below boiling point. Remove the pan from the heat and discard the tarragon. Transfer the vinegar to a heatproof bowl and beat in the egg yolks. Place the bowl over a pan of hot, but not boiling water and beat until the sauce thickens. Remove from the heat and beat in the butter a little at a time.

Transfer the fish to a large serving dish. Serve immediately, with the sauce in a sauceboat and accompanied by boiled potatoes or asparagus.

TURBOT WITH LOBSTER

Serves 6

1 x 1.5 kg/3 lb turbot
salt and freshly ground black pepper
65 g/2 oz butter
1/2 bottle sparkling white wine
1 small lobster
250 g/8 oz langoustines
1 shallot, peeled and chopped
1 small onion, peeled and chopped
8 tsp tomato purée
25 g/1 oz beurre manié, made by combining
  equal quantities of softened butter and flour
3 sprigs parsley

Preheat the oven to 170° C/325° F, gas mark 3.

Make several cuts in the black skin of the turbot and partially separate the fillets. Arrange the fish in a baking tin, sprinkle with salt, dot with 40 g/1 oz of the butter and pour over the wine. Bake for 30 minutes, or until tender.

Meanwhile, cook the lobster in boiling water for 15 minutes.

Peel the langoustines. Crush or mince the heads and shells.

Remove the baking tin from the oven and keep the turbot hot. Reserve the cooking juices.

Melt the remaining butter and fry the shallot and onion for 5-7 minutes, or until golden. Add the crushed langoustine shells and cook for 2-3 minutes. Stir in the tomato purée and turbot cooking juices. Simmer for 10 minutes. Rub the mixture through a wire strainer, season to taste and stir in the *beurre manié*, a little at a time, beating to incorporate thoroughly before adding the next piece.

Drain the lobster, twist off and crack the large claws and split the shell, using a sharp knife. Remove the sac, intestines and gills. Slice the tail meat into medallions. Arrange the turbot on a large serving dish, pour over the sauce and garnish with the lobster, langoustines and parsley.

Top: Roast Sea Bream (see page 26)
Bottom; Baked Sea-Bass

OILY FISH

SOUSED MACKEREL

Serves 6

1 onion, peeled and finely chopped
1 carrot, peeled and finely chopped
250 ml/8 fl oz white wine
100 ml/4 fl oz white wine vinegar
1 bay leaf
12 peppercorns
12 small mackerel or herring, cleaned

Put the onion, carrot, white wine, vinegar, bay leaf and peppercorns in a pressure cooker. Bring to HIGH pressure and cook for 15 minutes.

Allow the pressure to reduce at room temperature. Preheat the oven to 180° C/350° F, gas mark 4.

Place the fish in an ovenproof dish and pour over the vinegar mixture. Bake for 10-15 minutes.

Remove the dish from the oven and allow to cool. Marinate in the refrigerator for 2 days.

Serve accompanied by boiled potatoes and a tomato salad.

SEA-BASS SPECIAL

Serves 6

1 x 1 kg/2 lb sea-bass
250 g/8 oz mushrooms
100 g/3 oz butter
2 shallots, peeled and chopped
1 onion, peeled and chopped
2 truffles, sliced
100g/3 oz York ham, chopped
3 tbsp tomato purée
2 leeks, trimmed and sliced
2 carrots, peeled and chopped
2 tomatoes, skinned, seeded and chopped
1 celery stalk, trimmed and chopped
500 ml/17 fl oz white wine
500 g/1 lb clams
1 kg/2 lb mussels
salt and freshly ground black pepper
1 tsp cornflour
3 egg yolks
200 ml/7 fl oz single cream

Preheat the oven to 180° C/350° F, gas mark 4. Open the sea-bass on one side and remove the backbone without detaching the head. Set aside.

Finely chop the mushrooms and squeeze them in a clean cloth to remove all the moisture.

Melt 50 g/2 oz of the butter and sauté the shallots and 2 tbsp of the onion for 5-7 minutes. Add the mushrooms and truffles and cook for 3-5 minutes. Add the ham and tomato purée. Simmer for 5 minutes.

Stuff the fish with the mixture and secure the opening with fine string.

Arrange the leeks, carrots, tomatoes and celery in an ovenproof casserole. Place the sea-bass on top. Pour over half the wine and cook in the oven for about 25 minutes, or until tender.

Meanwhile, scrub the clams and mussels. Discard any that do not close when sharply tapped. Put them in a pan with the remaining wine and season with salt and pepper. (If more liquid is required, add cold water or fish stock.) Bring to the boil

Top: Soused Mackerel
Bottom: Sea-Bass Special

and cook until the shells have opened.

Remove the casserole from the oven and keep the fish warm. Strain the cooking liquid. Mix 1 tbsp of the liquid with the cornflour and heat the rest in a pan. Stir in the cornflour mixture, bring to the boil and cook, stirring until thickened. Remove from the heat. Beat in the egg yolks and the remaining butter.

Drain the shellfish. Discard any that have not opened. Set aside a few for the garnish. Remove the remainder from their shells.

Remove the string and skin the sea-bass. Arrange it on a large serving plate. Beat the cream, stir it into the sauce and pour over the fish. Garnish with the clams and mussels and decorate with those still in their shells. Serve immediately.

SARDINE SUPPER

Serves 4

1 kg/2 lb potatoes, peeled and thickly sliced
1 kg/2 lb fresh sardines, cleaned
50 g/2 oz flour
500 ml/17 fl oz vegetable oil

Cook the potatoes in boiling salted water for 15-20 minutes, or until tender. Drain and keep warm.

Meanwhile, scale the sardines and coat with flour. Heat the oil and fry them, in batches if necessary, until golden. Drain on absorbent paper.

Place the sardines on a large serving dish and arrange the potato slices around them. Sprinkle over a little of the cooking oil and serve immediately.

TROUT PARCELS

Serves 6

6 trout
60 g/2 oz butter
1 large onion, peeled and finely chopped
150 g/5 oz mushrooms, thinly sliced
50 g/2 oz blanched almonds, chopped
juice of 1 lemon
2 tbsp sherry
salt and freshly ground black pepper
6 small rosemary sprigs

Preheat the oven to 200° C/400° F, gas mark 6. Clean the trout and remove the backbones and eyes. Wash and pat dry. Set aside

To make the stuffing, melt 75 g/3 oz of the butter and fry the onion for 5-7 minutes, or until golden. Add the mushrooms and cook for 2-3 minutes over

low heat. Add the almonds, lemon juice and sherry. Season to taste.

Season the trout and divide the stuffing mixture between them. Close the fish and put a rosemary sprig on each one.

Cut six squares of aluminium foil large enough to enclose each fish. Melt the remaining butter and brush the foil with it. Place one fish on each foil square, fold over and seal the edges securely but not so tightly that the foil sticks to the fish.

Place the parcels on a baking sheet and bake for 20 minutes, or until the fish is tender. Serve immediately in the parcels.

SARDINES GYPSY-STYLE

Serves 4

16 fresh sardines, cleaned
1/2 loaf made into breadcrumbs
140-225 ml/5-8 fl oz milk
1 tbsp vegetable oil
1 large onion, peeled and chopped
2 garlic cloves, peeled and chopped
1 tbsp chopped parsley
salt and freshly ground black pepper
50 g/2 oz flour
2 eggs, lightly beaten
oil for deep-frying

Scale the sardines. Remove their heads and backbones and set the fish aside.

Place the breadcrumbs in a bowl and pour over just enough milk to cover. Set aside to soak.

Heat the vegetable oil and fry the onion for 5-7 minutes, or until golden. Add the garlic and parsley and cook for 2-3 minutes. Remove the pan from the heat and drain off the oil.

Drain the breadcrumbs and stir them into the onion mixture.

Heat the deep-frying oil to 190° C/ 375° F or until a cube of stale bread turns golden in 30 seconds.

Place eight of the sardines on a work surface and season well. Cover them with the onion and breadcrumb mixture. Top each sardine with another to make a 'sandwich'. Coat each 'sandwich' first in flour and then in beaten egg and fry in hot oil until golden, crisp and cooked through.

Drain on absorbent paper and transfer to a large serving plate. Serve very hot accompanied by a green salad.

SEA-BASS CHOUX

Serves 8

1 x 2 kg/4 lb sea-bass, cleaned
salt and freshly ground white pepper

pinch grated nutmeg
50 g/1 lb Mediterranean prawns, peeled and deveined, shells and heads reserved
50 g/2 oz butter
40 g/1 oz flour
200 ml/7 fl oz milk
2 eggs, lightly beaten
225 ml/8 fl oz white wine
Choux paste:
35 g/1 oz butter
150 ml/5 fl oz water
salt
75 g/3 oz flour, sifted
2 eggs, lightly beaten

Glaze:
1 egg, lightly beaten

Remove and reserve the fish's backbone. Wash the fish, pat dry and season with salt, pepper and grated nutmeg. Set aside.

Put the prawn shells and fish bone in a pan, cover with water, season and bring to the boil. Simmer for 15 minutes.

Slice the prawn tails and set aside. Work the prawn heads with half the butter in a blender until smooth.

Melt the prawn-flavoured butter and stir in the flour. Cook, stirring, for 1 minute. Remove the pan from the heat and gradually stir in the milk. Return to the heat and bring to the boil, stirring. Simmer, stirring, for 1-2 minutes, or until thick and smooth. Remove the pan from the heat and beat in the eggs. Stir in the reserved prawns and season.

Strain the fish stock and reserve.

Stuff the sea-bass with the prawn mixture and secure the opening with fine string. Place the fish in a fish kettle or flameproof casserole, dot with the remaining butter and pour over the wine and the reserved fish stock. Place on moderately high heat, cover and cook for 30 minutes, checking from time to time that it is not overcooked.

Remove the kettle from the heat and set the fish aside to cool in the cooking liquid. Preheat the oven to 200° C/400° F, gas mark 6.

Meanwhile make the choux paste. Put the butter, water and a pinch of salt in a pan over low heat and stir gently until the butter has melted. Add the flour and beat the mixture until it comes away from the sides of the pan. Gradually beat in the eggs until the dough is smooth and glossy. Set aside.

Remove the fish from the stock, remove and discard the string and skin. Arrange it on a baking sheet and cover with the choux paste. Using the point of a teaspoon, make a pattern of fish scales over

Right: Sea-Bass Choux

the paste. Brush with beaten egg and bake in the oven for about 10 minutes, or until the pastry is golden.

Transfer the fish to a large serving dish and serve immediately accompanied by asparagus.

GRILLED SALMON

Serves 6

6 slices fresh salmon
salt and freshly ground white pepper

Marinade:
100 ml/4 fl oz vegetable oil
1 large onion, peeled and chopped
1 parsley sprig
juice of 1 lemon

First make the marinade. Mix together the oil, onion, parsley and lemon juice.

Season the salmon and arrange in a single layer in a large dish. Pour over the marinade and set aside for 1 hour, turning the fish over from time to time.

Preheat the grill.

Arrange the fish on the grill rack and cook, brushing with the marinade from time to time, for 4-5 minutes on each side, or until tender.

Serve immediately, accompanied by boiled potatoes and, if liked, mayonnaise.

SALMON PARCELS

Serves 6

4 carrots, peeled
4 leeks, trimmed
1 celery stalk, trimmed
75 g/3 oz butter
250 ml/8 fl oz white wine
salt and freshly ground white pepper
100 ml/4 fl oz single cream
6 salmon steaks

Cut the carrots, leeks and celery into matchstick strips. Melt 50 g/2oz of the butter and sauté the carrots for 5 minutes. Add the leeks and celery and cook for a further 5 minutes. Stir in the wine, cover and cook for 10 minutes.

Meanwhile, preheat the oven to 200° C/400° F, gas mark 6.

Season the vegetable mixture and stir in the cream. Remove the pan from the heat and set aside.

Cut six squares of aluminium foil each large enough to enclose a salmon steak. Melt the remaining butter and brush over the foil squares. Place a salmon steak on each piece of foil and divide the vegetable mixture between them. Fold over the foil and seal the edges.

Place the parcels on a baking sheet and cook in the oven for 15 minutes, or until tender.

Serve immediately in the parcels, taking care not to tear them so that you do not lose any of the sauce.

Far left: Grilled Salmon
Left: Salmon Parcels

TUNA WITH SAFFRON

Serves 6

1 kg/2 lb fresh tuna
50 ml/2 fl oz vegetable oil
2 garlic cloves, peeled and chopped
500 g/1 lb potatoes, peeled and sliced
1/2 tsp saffron threads
salt
2 tsp chopped fresh thyme or 1/2 tsp dried thyme
250 ml/8 fl oz lager
40 g/1 oz butter, sliced

Preheat the oven to 170° C/325° F, gas
mark 3. Cut the tuna into medium-sized
slices and set aside.

Heat the oil in a flameproof casserole
and fry the garlic for 3-4 minutes, or until
golden. Remove the casserole from the
heat. Arrange the potato slices and the
tuna in the casserole. Pound the saffron
with a little salt in a mortar. Sprinkle the
saffron mixture and the thyme over the
tuna. Pour over the beer, cover and cook
in the oven for about 50 minutes.

Remove the casserole from the oven
and add the butter. Return to the oven for
a further 10 minutes, or until the butter
has melted.

Serve immediately straight from
the casserole.

BUTTERED TROUT

Serves 6

6 trout
225 ml/8 fl oz milk
1 tsp salt
3 tbsp flour
125 g/4 oz butter
juice of 1 lemon
1 tbsp chopped parsley
freshly ground black pepper
1 lemon, thinly sliced
6 parsley sprigs

Wash the trout and pat dry. Season the
milk with the salt. Dip the fish in the milk
and coat with the flour.

Melt the butter in a frying-pan and fry
the trout over moderate heat for about 20
minutes, or until golden.

Arrange the trout on a large serving
dish. Sprinkle over the lemon juice, the
butter from the frying-pan, the chopped
parsley and pepper to taste. Garnish with
lemon and parsley and serve immediately.

**Top: Squid in its own ink (see
page 55)**
Bottom: Tuna with Saffron

SALMON TROUT WITH HAM

Serves 6

6 salmon trout, cleaned
salt and freshly ground white pepper
3 lemons
8 thick slices ham
25 g/1 oz flour
4 tbsp vegetable oil
50 g/2 oz butter

Remove the backbones and eyes from the
fish. Wash and pat dry. Season the fish and
sprinkle over the juice of 1 lemon.

Cut the ham into thin strips. Reserve
one-quarter and divide the remainder
between the fish cavities. Secure them
with cocktail sticks and coat with flour.

Heat the oil and fry the trout for 15-20
minutes, or until they are golden
and tender.

Finely chop the reserved ham. Melt the
butter and sauté the ham for 3-5 minutes.
Stir in the juice of the remaining lemons
and set aside.

Arrange the salmon trout on a large
serving dish and garnish with the hot ham
mixture. Serve immediately, accompanied
by boiled potatoes.

BONITO IN WHITE WINE

Serves 4

1 kg/2 lb bonito
salt and freshly ground black pepper
25 g/1 oz flour
4 tbsp vegetable oil
1 large onion, peeled and finely chopped
2 garlic cloves, peeled and finely chopped
2 large green peppers, seeded and thinly sliced
250 ml/8 fl oz white wine
parsley sprigs

Cut the fish into slices. Season with salt
and pepper and coat with the flour.

Heat 3 tbsp of the oil and fry the fish for
5 minutes on each side, or until golden.
Drain the fish and transfer to an ovenproof
casserole. Reserve the oil.

Preheat the oven to 180° C/350° F, gas
mark 4.

Heat the remaining oil and fry the onion
and garlic for 4-5 minutes, or until soft.
Add the peppers and cook over low heat
for 5-7 minutes, or until soft. Add the
vegetables to the casserole.

Add the wine to the pan in which the
fish was cooked and bring to the boil.
Allow to reduce slightly, then pour over
the fish. Bake in the oven for about 20
minutes, or until tender. Serve in the
casserole, garnished with the parsley sprigs.

STUFFED BAKED FISH

Serves 6

1 kg/2 lb large, fresh sardines or small fresh
herring
3 tbsp vegetable oil
125 g/3 oz breadcrumbs
25 g/1 oz pine nuts
1 tbsp chopped parsley
1 canned anchovy, drained and chopped
pinch grated nutmeg
freshly ground black pepper
4-5 bay leaves, torn into small pieces
juice of 1 lemon

Clean the fish and remove the backbones
and heads. Wash the fish and spread them
out, open, on a work surface.

Heat 1 tbsp of the oil and add the
breadcrumbs, pine nuts, parsley, anchovy,
nutmeg and pepper to taste. Mix well and
remove from the heat. Stir in 1 tbsp of the
remaining oil.

Put a spoonful of the stuffing in each of
the prepared fish. Close the cavities. Brush
a baking tin with the remaining oil and
arrange the fish in rows side-by-side. Insert
a small piece of bay leaf between each fish.
Sprinkle over the remaining breadcrumbs
and bake for 30 minutes, or until tender.

Arrange the fish on a large serving dish,
sprinkle over the lemon juice and serve.

BONITO WITH VEGETABLES

Serves 6

1 large aubergine, sliced
salt and freshly ground black pepper
1 kg/2 lb bonito fillets
100 g/3 oz flour
3 eggs, lightly beaten
155-200 ml/5-7 fl oz vegetable oil
2 potatoes, peeled and sliced
1 large onion, peeled and cut into matchstick
strips
2 tomatoes, skinned, seeded and chopped
3 eggs
juice of 1 lemon
50 g/2 oz green olives, stoned and sliced

Preheat the oven to 190° C/375° F, gas
mark 5.

Place the aubergine slices in a shallow
dish and cover with lightly salted water.
Leave to soak to remove the bitterness.

Season the fish, coat with flour and dip
in the beaten egg. Heat 50 ml/2 fl oz of
the oil and fry the fish until golden on
both sides. Drain and set aside.

Heat 50 ml/2 fl oz of the remaining oil
and fry the potato slices until golden on
both sides. Drain on and set aside.

Drain the aubergine slices, rinse and pat dry. Coat them in flour. Heat 25 ml/ 1 fl oz of the remaining oil and fry them until golden on both sides, adding more oil if required. Drain and set aside.

Heat 1 tbsp of the remaining oil and sauté the onion for 2-3 minutes. Drain and set aside.

Rub the tomatoes through a wire sieve or work in a blender to make a purée.

Arrange the fried vegetables and the fish in a large, ovenproof casserole and pour over the puréed tomato. Cover and bake for 10 minutes, or until tender.

Remove the casserole from the oven, sprinkle over the lemon juice and olives and serve immediately.

SEA GREEN DELIGHT

Serves 8

1 x 1.5 kg/3 lb sea-bass, cleaned and scaled
salt and freshly ground black pepper
2 lemons
50 g/2 oz butter
100 ml/4 fl oz fish stock
100 ml/4 fl oz white wine
8 cooked Mediterranean prawns or langoustines
4 hard-boiled eggs, shelled and sliced

Green sauce:
250 g/8 oz spinach
1 parsley sprig
2 egg yolks
salt and freshly ground black pepper
260 ml/9 fl oz olive oil
1 tbsp lemon juice

Preheat the oven to 180° C/350° F, gas mark 4.

Remove the fish's backbone without detaching the head, Sprinkle salt, pepper and the juice of 1 lemon inside the fish and insert a knob of butter. Close the cavity. Lightly grease a baking tin and place the fish in it. Sprinkle with salt and bake for about 10 minutes, or until the skin puffs up.

Remove the tin from the oven and skin the fish. Melt the remaining butter. Return the fish to the baking tin and pour over the stock, wine, the juice of the remaining lemon and the melted butter. Return to the oven and cook for 30 minutes, or until tender.

Meanwhile make the sauce. Rinse the spinach and parsley and cook in the water clinging to the leaves for about 7 minutes, or until tender. Drain and squeeze out

Left: Bonito with Vegetables
Right: Sea Green Delight

excess moisture. Rub through a fine wire sieve or work in a blender or food processor and set aside.

Beat together the egg yolks and seasoning. Beat in the oil, drop by drop, until half has been incorporated. Add the remainder in a thin stream, beating constantly. Alternatively, make the mayonnaise in a blender, working the mixture all the time and adding the oil in a thin stream. Add the lemon juice. Mix the spinach mixture with the mayonnaise and set aside.

Transfer the fish to a large serving dish. Pour over the sauce and garnish with the shellfish and hard-boiled eggs.

FISH LOAF

Serves 6

500 g/1 lb bonito
5 tbsp breadcrumbs
1 egg
170 ml/6 fl oz white wine
salt
pinch grated nutmeg
15 g/ oz butter
175 g/6 oz bacon, rinds removed

Garnish:
lettuce
1 bunch young asparagus, cooked, or 1 can asparagus, drained
3 hard-boiled eggs, shelled and halved
6 tsp lumpfish roe (mock caviar)
6 thin slices carrot
6 tsp mayonnaise

Preheat the oven to 180° C/350° F, gas mark 4.

Finely chop the fish, removing any bones. Mix the fish, 2 tbsp of the breadcrumbs, the raw egg and wine. Season with salt and nutmeg to taste.

Grease the sides and bottom of a loaf tin with the butter and sprinkle over the remaining breadcrumbs. Place a layer of the fish mixture in the bottom of the tin and smooth the surface. Cover with a layer of bacon, then add another layer of fish mixture. Continue making layers until all the ingredients have been used up.

Cook in the oven for 30 minutes, or until cooked through.

Remove the tin from the oven and allow the loaf to cool without removing it from the tin.

To serve, turn out the loaf and cut into thick slices. Make a bed of shredded lettuce on a large serving plate and arrange the slices on top. Garnish with asparagus, hard-boiled eggs, lumpfish roe and carrot slices and serve with mayonnaise, if liked.

SARDINES WITH GARLIC AND PARSLEY

Serves 6

1 kg/2 lb fresh sardines, cleaned
salt
100 ml/4 fl oz vegetable oil
4 garlic cloves, peeled and thinly sliced
1 tbsp chopped parsley
100 ml/4 fl oz white wine
2 tbsp breadcrumbs
1 lemon, cut into wedges

Preheat the oven to 180° C/350° F, gas mark 4.

Remove the skin and backbones from the fish. Wash, drain and season with salt.

Heat the oil in a flameproof casserole. Fry the garlic and parsley for 3–5 minutes until the garlic is just golden. Add the sardines and twirl the dish vigorously. Add the wine, sprinkle over the breadcrumbs and cook in the oven for about 12 minutes, or until tender.

Serve immediately in the casserole, garnished with lemon wedges.

TROUT IN RED WINE

Serves 6

2 litres/3 pints water
500 ml/17 fl oz red wine
2 carrots, peeled and cut into matchstick strips
1 onion, peeled and thinly sliced
1 bay leaf
1 tbsp chopped parsley
12 black peppercorns
6 trout
4 tbsp red wine vinegar
100 ml/4 fl oz single cream
salt

Put the water, wine, carrots, onion, bay leaf, parsley and peppercorns in a large pan and bring to the boil. Cover and simmer for 30 minutes.

Clean the trout. Heat the vinegar and sprinkle it over the fish. Set aside for 5 minutes.

Strain the red wine stock. Drain the trout and arrange in a single layer in a large pan or fish kettle. Pour over the stock, cover and poach for 15 minutes, or until tender.

Drain the trout, reserving the cooking liquid. Skin the fish and arrange them on a large serving dish.

Bring the reserved cooking liquid to the boil and reduce slightly. Stir in the cream, add salt to taste and pour over the fish. Serve immediately, accompanied by boiled potatoes.

TUNA MOULD

Serves 6

1 kg/2 lb potatoes, peeled and cut into chunks
salt and freshly ground white pepper
50 g/2 oz butter
50 ml/2 fl oz milk
4 tomatoes, skinned, seeded and sliced
250 g/8 oz canned tuna
50 ml/2 fl oz vegetable oil
1 large onion, peeled and finely chopped
1 egg, lightly beaten

Garnish:
lettuce leaves
140 ml/5 fl oz mayonnaise
1 red pepper, seeded, blanched and cut into strips
2 hard-boiled eggs, shelled and sliced

Cook the potatoes in plenty of boiling salted water for 15–20 minutes, or until tender. Drain and mash with half the butter and the milk. Season with salt and pepper and set aside.

Melt the remaining butter and fry the tomatoes for 5–8 minutes, or until soft. Rub through a wire sieve or work in a blender or food processor until a smooth purée is formed.

Drain and flake the tuna.

Heat half the oil and fry the onion for 5 minutes, or until it is soft. Stir in the fried tomato purée and the tuna. Remove from the heat and work the mixture in a food processor or blender until fully incorporated.

Beat the fish mixture into the mashed potato. Beat in the egg. Taste and adjust the seasoning.

Brush a ring mould with the remaining oil. Pour in the fish and potato mixture, spreading it out evenly and smoothing the top. Allow to cool completely, then chill in the refrigerator for at least 3 hours and preferably overnight.

To serve, turn the mould out on to a large serving dish. Line the centre of the ring with lettuce leaves and fill with mayonnaise. Garnish with the pepper strips and hard-boiled eggs.

OTHER DISHES

GREEK FROGS' LEGS

Serves 6

18 pairs frogs' legs,
2.25 litres/4 pints water
250 ml/8 fl oz milk
100 g/3 oz butter
1 carrot, peeled and sliced
1 onion, peeled and chopped
1 leek, trimmed and sliced
250 ml/8 fl oz white wine
1 tbsp flour
salt and freshly ground white pepper
pinch grated nutmeg
4 egg yolks, lightly beaten with 2 tbsp water
1 tbsp chopped parsley

Wash and trim the frogs' legs. Mix 2
litres/3 pints of the water and the milk
together and soak the frogs' legs in this
mixture for 1 hour. Drain and set aside.

Melt 20 g/ oz of the butter and fry the
carrot, onion and leek for 5 minutes, or
until soft but not coloured. Stir in the
wine and the remaining water. Season
with salt and pepper to taste and add the
parsley. Add the frogs' legs and simmer
until tender, testing by gently piercing the
thighs with a fork.

Drain the frogs' legs and set aside. Strain
the cooking liquid and reserve.

To make the sauce, melt the remaining
butter. Stir in the flour and cook, stirring,
for 1 minute. Remove the pan from the
heat and stir in 250 ml/8 fl oz of the
reserved cooking liquid. Return to the
heat and bring to the boil, stirring.
Simmer, stirring, for 1-2 minutes, or until
smooth. Season with salt and pepper and
stir in the nutmeg. Beat in the egg yolk
mixture and and add the frogs' legs. Heat
gently without boiling.

Transfer to a large serving dish, sprinkle
over the parsley and serve immediately.

SEAFOOD SYMPHONY

Serves 6

6 langoustines
6 large clams
6 mussels
100 g/3 oz butter
1 onion, peeled and chopped
2 garlic cloves, peeled and crushed
1 tbsp chopped parsley

250 ml/8 fl oz brandy
8 tbsp tomato purée
300 ml/10 fl oz stock or water
25 g/1 oz beurre manié, made by blending
  equal quantities of softened butter and flour
freshly ground black pepper

Top: Tuna Mould
Bottom: Greek Frogs' Legs

2 x 150 g/5 oz sole, filleted and sliced
250 g/8 oz squid, cleaned and chopped
250 g/8 oz cod fillets, sliced
250 g/8 oz mackerel fillets, sliced

Peel and chop the langoustines, reserving the shells. Crush the shells in a mortar or work in a food processor and set aside.

Scrub the clams and mussels under cold running water and discard any that do not shut when sharply tapped. Set aside in cold water.

Melt the butter and fry the onion and garlic for 7-8 minutes. Add the parsley and langoustine shells and cook for 5 minutes. Stir in the brandy and warm gently. Ignite it and shake the pan gently until the flames die down.

Add the tomato purée and stock or water and bring to the boil. Beat in the *beurre manié*, a little at a time. Continue beating until each piece is incorporated before adding the next. Season with pepper.

Gently stir the langoustines, sole, squid, cod and mackerel into the sauce. Add the clams and mussels and cook for 5-10 minutes, or until the fish is tender and the shellfish have opened. Discard any clams or mussels that have not opened.

Transfer the mixture to a large serving dish and serve immediately.

FRIED FISH MIX

Serves 6

250 ml/8 fl oz olive oil
1 tbsp cayenne pepper
salt and freshly ground white pepper
6 hake fillets
250 ml/8 fl oz white wine
juice of 1 lemon
1 tbsp chopped parsley
6 John Dory fillets
500 g/1 lb squid
500 g/1 lb fresh anchovies
200 g/7 oz flour
100 g/3 oz breadcrumbs
170 ml/6 fl oz vegetable oil
1 lemon, cut into wedges

Make a marinade by mixing together the olive oil, cayenne pepper and a little salt. Cut the hake into strips, immerse in the marinade and set aside for at least 1 hour.

Make another marinade with the wine, half the lemon juice, salt and parsley. Cut the John Dory into strips, immerse in the marinade and set aside for at least 1 hour.

Clean the squid and cut into rings. Sprinkle with salt and the remaining lemon juice and set aside.

Clean the anchovies and remove the heads and backbones. Wash and drain. Season with salt and pepper.

Drain the hake, coat with breadcrumbs and set aside. Drain the John Dory, coat with flour and set aside.

Divide the vegetable oil between two frying-pans and heat it. Coat the squid in equal quantities of flour and breadcrumbs and fry until golden and tender. Drain on absorbent paper.

At the same time, fry the John Dory in the other pan until golden and tender. Drain on absorbent paper.

Coat the anchovies with flour and fry in the first pan until crisp and golden. Drain on absorbent paper.

Meanwhile, fry the hake in the second pan until golden and tender. Drain on absorbent paper.

Heap the fish on a serving plate, garnish with the lemon wedges and serve immediately.

SEAFOOD ROLL

Serves 6

6 eggs
3 tbsp cornflour
3 tbsp flour, sifted
salt

Filling:
50 g/2 oz butter
50 g/2 oz flour
500 ml/17 fl oz fish stock
250 g/8 oz hake fillets, chopped
250 g/8 oz cod, chopped
250 g/8 oz prawns, peeled and deveined

Topping:
6 tbsp thick mayonnaise
6 langoustines, peeled

Preheat the oven to 180° C/350° F, gas mark 4. Line a Swiss roll tin with non-stick silicone paper or greased greaseproof paper.

First make the filling. Melt the butter and stir in the flour. Cook, stirring, for 1 minute. Remove from the heat and stir in the stock. Return to the heat and bring to the boil, stirring. Simmer, stirring, for 1-2 minutes, or until thick and smooth. Add the fish and prawns and cook for 5-10 minutes, or until tender. Set aside.

To make the sponge roll, beat the eggs until thick. Fold in the cornflour, flour and a pinch of salt. Spread the mixture in the prepared tin and bake for 10 minutes.

Remove the baking tin from the oven and turn the sponge out on to a clean cloth. Spread with the filling and roll up, Swiss Roll style, using the cloth to help. Set aside to cool.

When the roll is cold, cover it with mayonnaise and cut crossways into slices. Decorate with the langoustines and serve immediately.

FISH RING WITH RICE

Serves 6

300 g/10 oz hake fillets
300 g/10 oz cod fillets
50 g/2 oz butter
salt and freshly ground black pepper
200 g/7 oz long-grain rice
200 g/7 oz prawns, peeled and deveined
1 tsp vegetable oil
500 g/1 lb mushrooms, thinly sliced
75 ml/3 fl oz water
1 lemon slice, peeled
1 tbsp made mustard

Tartare sauce:
250 ml/8 fl oz mayonnaise
2 hard-boiled egg yolks, finely chopped
5 gherkins, finely chopped
25 g/1 oz capers, finely chopped
1 tsp made mustard
salt and freshly ground white pepper

Preheat the oven to 180° C/350° F, gas mark 4.

Cut the hake and the cod into thin slices, using a sharp knife with a thin blade. Put the fish slices, butter and a little salt in an ovenproof dish and bake for 10 minutes, or until the fish is tender.

Rinse the rice in cold water and then cook in plenty of boiling, salted water for 15 minutes, or until tender.

To make the tartare sauce, thoroughly mix together the mayonnaise, egg yolks, gherkins and capers. Stir in mustard and seasoning to taste.

Remove the fish from the oven.

Reserve a few prawns for decoration and stir the remainder into the fish mixture.

Drain the rice and rinse with boiling water two or three times. Allow to cool slightly and then mix with a little tartare sauce to bind it .

Brush a ring mould with the vegetable oil. Fill the mould with the fish mixture and the rice, smoothing the top. Set aside to cool completely.

Meanwhile, cook the mushrooms with the water, lemon, mustard and pepper for 2-3 minutes. Set aside to cool.

To serve, unmould on to a large serving plate. Fill the ring with the mushrooms and decorate with the reserved prawns. Serve the tartare sauce separately.

Top: Turbot with Lobster (see page 34)
Bottom: Fish Ring with Rice

DEEP-FRIED FROGS' LEGS

Serves 6

18 pairs frogs' legs
250 ml/8 fl oz milk
2 litres/3 pints water
250 ml/8 fl oz olive oil
juice of 2 lemons
2 garlic cloves, peeled and chopped
2 tbsp chopped parsley
salt and freshly ground white pepper
250 g/8 oz flour
4 eggs, lightly beaten
oil for deep-frying

Wash and trim the frogs' legs. Mix together the milk and water and soak the frogs' legs in this mixture for 1 hour.

Make a marinade by mixing together the olive oil, lemon juice, garlic, parsley, salt and pepper. Drain the frogs' legs and marinate them , turning them from time to time, for 2-3 hours.

Heat the oil in a deep-fryer to 190° C/ 375° F or until a cube of stale bread turns golden in 30 seconds.

Drain the frogs' legs. Coat first with flour and then with beaten egg. Deep-fry, in batches if necessary, until golden and cooked through.

Serve immediately.

BABY EELS BASQUE-STYLE

Serves 2

2 tbsp vegetable oil
2 garlic cloves, peeled and thinly sliced
½ chili pepper, seeded
200 g/7 oz baby eels

Heat the oil in a flameproof earthenware dish★ and fry the garlic and chili pepper for 5-8 minutes, or until the garlic is golden. During cooking, rub the chili pepper against the base of the dish with a wooden spatula.

Remove the dish from the heat and allow to cool until tepid.

Remove and discard the chili pepper. Add the eels and return to high heat. Cook, stirring with a wooden spatula to coat the eels with the flavoured oil.

Continue cooking and stirring until the oil is just below boiling point.

Remove the dish from the heat, cover with a lid and serve immediately.

★ A traditional Spanish *cazuela* is ideal. In Spain, special wooden forks may be used for eating this boiling hot dish to avoid burning the mouth.

Left: Fish Loaf (see page 44)
Below: Deep-fried frogs' legs

SHELLFISH

SNAILS IN HERB SAUCE

Serves 6

500 ml/17 fl oz vegetable oil
1 onion, peeled and chopped
6 garlic cloves, peeled and chopped
250 g/8 oz ham, minced
2 kg/4 lb cooked snails, thawed if frozen
salt and freshly ground black pepper
2 tbsp chopped parsley
1 bay leaf
1 tsp chopped thyme or 1/2 tsp dried thyme
1/2 tsp ground cloves
1/2 tsp ground cumin
225 ml/8 fl oz tomato purée
225 ml/8 fl oz stock

Heat the oil and fry the onion and garlic for 5-8 minutes, or until they are beginning to turn golden. Add the ham and the snails, season well with salt and pepper and stir in the herbs and spices. Add the tomato purée and sufficient stock to cover. Cook over low heat for 5 minutes, or until heated through.

Discard the bay leaf, transfer the mixture to a serving bowl and serve immediately.

CURRIED MUSSELS

Serves 4

1 kg/2 lb mussels
250 ml/8 fl oz water
250 ml/8 fl oz white wine
50 g/2 oz butter
1 onion, peeled and finely chopped
20 g/ oz flour
2 tomatoes, skinned, seeded and finely chopped
1 tbsp Madras curry powder
250 ml/8 fl oz single cream
salt and freshly ground black pepper

Scrub the mussels in cold running water, discarding any which do not shut when sharply tapped. Put them in a pan with the water and wine and bring to the boil. Cook until the shells open.

Drain the mussels, reserving the cooking liquid. Discard any closed shells. Remove the mussels from their shells and set aside. Strain the cooking liquid through clean muslin to remove any grit and reserve.

Melt the butter and sauté the onion for 5-8 minutes, or until it is just beginning to turn golden. Stir in the tomatoes, cover and cook over low heat for 10 minutes, or until the mixture forms a purée.

Stir in the curry powder, the reserved cooking liquid and the cream. Season to taste. Add the mussels and bring the mixture to just below boiling point. Serve immediately.

GRATIN OF CLAMS

Serves 6

1 kg/2 lb large clams
50 g/2 oz butter
1 onion, peeled and finely chopped
1 tbsp flour
170 ml/6 fl oz white wine
200 g/7 oz mushrooms, chopped
2 tbsp tomato purée
1 tbsp capers
lemon juice
salt and freshly ground white pepper
125 g/4 oz Parmesan cheese, grated

Scrub the clams under cold running water. Discard any that do not shut when sharply tapped. Put them in a pan, cover with water and bring to the boil. Cook until the shells open. Drain the clams. Discard any that are still closed. Remove from their shells and reserve.

Preheat the oven to 200° C/400° F, gas mark 6.

Melt the butter and sauté the onion for 5 minutes. Stir in the flour and cook, stirring, for 2 minutes. Remove from the heat and stir in the wine. Return to the heat and bring to the boil, stirring. Add the mushrooms and simmer for 5 minutes.

Heat the tomato purée, stir in the capers and lemon juice and season to taste.

Stir the clams into the wine sauce and transfer to an ovenproof dish. Pour over the tomato and caper mixture, sprinkle with the grated cheese and bake in the oven for 8 minutes, or until golden.

Serve immediately.

DIJON MUSSELS

Serves 6

1.5 kg/3 lb mussels
50 ml/2 fl oz vegetable oil
1 onion, peeled and finely chopped
1 tsp flour
1 tbsp Dijon mustard
salt and freshly ground black pepper
2 tbsp brandy
1 tbsp chopped parsley

Scrub the mussels under cold running water. Discard any that do not shut when sharply tapped. Place the mussels in a pan and add just enough water to cover. Bring to the boil and cook until the shells open.

Drain the mussels and reserve the cooking liquid. Remove the mussels from their shells. Discard any that have not opened. Set aside. Strain the cooking liquid through clean muslin to remove any grit, and reserve.

Heat the oil and sauté the onion for 5 minutes. Stir in the flour and cook, stirring for 2 minutes. Remove from the heat and stir in the reserved cooking liquid and mustard to taste. Return to the heat and bring to the boil, stirring. Simmer, stirring, for 1-2 minutes, or until smooth.

Season and stir in the brandy and the parsley. Add the mussels, cover and bring to the boil. Serve immediately.

GALICIAN OCTOPUS

Serves 6

1 kg/2 lb octopus
140 ml/5 fl oz brandy
2 garlic cloves, peeled and thinly sliced
2 tbsp olive oil
sea salt
1 tbsp paprika

Clean the octopus and remove the eyes and beaks. Rinse under cold running water for 10 minutes. Drain and beat well to tenderize. Blanch in boiling water. Drain.

Transfer the octopus to a pressure cooker and add water to cover. Bring to HIGH pressure and cook for 30 minutes.

Allow the pressure to reduce at room temperature. Open the cooker, add the brandy and cook for 3-4 minutes. Drain and cut the octopus into even-sized pieces. Set aside in a shallow dish.

Mix together the garlic, olive oil, sea salt and paprika to taste. Pour over the octopus and set aside to marinate for at least 1 hour.

This is traditionally served on a wooden platter with boiled potatoes and a cold or warm tomato salad.

Above: Galician Octopus
Below: Halibut in Prawn and Brandy Sauce (see page 18)

COLD CLAMS

Serves 6

1 kg/2 lb clams
2 tomatoes, skinned, seeded and chopped
1 hard-boiled egg, shelled and chopped
2 canned anchovies, drained and chopped
4 tbsp olive oil
2 tbsp white wine vinegar
1 tsp mustard
salt and freshly ground white pepper

Scrub the clams under cold running water, discarding any that do not close immediately when sharply tapped. Place in a pan, cover with water and bring to the boil. Cook until the shells open.

Drain the clams and remove from their shells, discarding any that have not opened. Set aside in a shallow dish.

Mix together the tomatoes, egg, anchovies, oil, vinegar and mustard. Season to taste. Pour over the clams and serve cold.

CLAMS A LA MARINIERE

Serves 4

1 kg/2 lb clams
100 ml/4 fl oz vegetable oil
1 onion, peeled and finely chopped
2 garlic cloves, peeled and finely chopped
1 tbsp tomato purée
2 tbsp breadcrumbs
225 ml/8 fl oz white wine
juice of 1 lemon
1 bay leaf
salt and freshly ground white pepper
1 tbsp chopped parsley

Scrub the clams under cold running water. Discard any that do not shut when sharply tapped. Place in a pan, cover with water and boil until the shells open.

Drain and reserve. Discard any that have not opened. Strain the cooking liquid through muslin to remove any grit.

Heat the oil and sauté the onion and garlic for 5–8 minutes. Stir in the tomato purée, breadcrumbs, wine and lemon juice. Cook for 5 minutes. Stir in the reserved liquid. Add the bay leaf, clams and seasoning. Simmer for 10 minutes.

Transfer to a serving dish, sprinkle over the parsley and serve immediately.

FRIED MUSSELS BECHAMEL

Serves 6

1 kg/2 lb large mussels
250 ml/8 fl oz white wine
250 ml/8 fl oz water
100 g/3 oz butter
100 g/3 oz flour
330 ml/11 fl oz milk
salt and freshly ground white pepper
1/2 tsp grated nutmeg
1 tbsp vegetable oil
oil for deep-frying

Coating:
100 g/3 oz flour
3 eggs, lightly beaten
170 g/6 oz breadcrumbs

Scrub the mussels under running water. Discard any that do not shut when sharply tapped. Place in a pan, pour over the wine and water and boil until they open.

Drain and discard any mussels that have not opened. Remove one shell from each mussel. Strain the cooking liquid through clean muslin to remove any grit, and reserve 250 ml/8 fl oz.

Top: Cold Clams
Bottom: Clams à la Marinière

Melt the butter and stir in the flour. Cook, stirring, for 1 minute. Remove from the heat and stir in the milk and reserved liquid. Return to the heat and simmer, stirring, for 10 minutes. Add salt, pepper and nutmeg. Set aside.

Brush a baking sheet with the oil. Dip the mussels in the sauce and coat well. Set aside to cool on the baking sheet.

When cold, coat them in flour, then egg and then breadcrumbs. Heat the deep-frying oil to 190° C/375° F or until a cube of stale bread turns golden in 30 seconds. Deep-fry the mussels until golden. Drain. and serve immediately.

CUTTLEFISH WITH APPLE

Serves 6

1 kg/2 lb cuttlefish or squid
50 g/2 oz flour
225 ml/8 fl oz vegetable oil
170 ml/6 fl oz brandy
2 garlic cloves, peeled and finely chopped
1 large onion, peeled and finely chopped
1 tbsp paprika
2 tomatoes, skinned, seeded and finely chopped
2 firm, sweet dessert apples, peeled and sliced
juice of 1 lemon
1 tbsp chopped parsley
2 tsp chopped thyme or tsp dried thyme
1 bay leaf
salt and freshly ground black pepper

Clean the cuttlefish or squid. Beat well to tenderize. Chop the tentacles and use to stuff the bodies. Secure with cocktail sticks. Coat with half the flour.

Heat half the oil and fry the cuttlefish or squid over high heat until golden. Lower the heat, pour over the brandy and ignite. Shake the pan gently until the flames die down. Remove the cocktail sticks, place the fish in a large pan and set aside.

Heat the remaining oil and fry the garlic for 5 minutes. Add the onion, cover and cook over low heat for 10 minutes,.

Stir in the paprika and remaining flour and cook, stirring for 2 minutes. Add the tomatoes, apples, lemon juice, parsley, thyme and bay leaf. Season with salt and pepper. Cover and cook for 30 minutes.

Remove the bay leaf and purée the mixture in a blender or food processor.

Pour the purée over the cuttlefish or squid, cover and cook over low heat for 30 minutes, or until the fish is tender.

Transfer to a large serving dish and serve immediately.

Right top: Crispy Cod Balls (see page 26)
Right bottom: Cuttlefish with Apple

LOBSTER MEDALLIONS

Serves 6

500 ml/17 fl oz water
1 envelope gelatine
4 hard-boiled eggs, shelled and halved
8 tsp lumpfish roe (mock caviar)
4 small cooked lobsters
2 truffles, sliced or 16 black olives, stoned and halved
170 ml/6 fl oz mayonnaise
6 small gherkins, chopped
6 small tomatoes
1 lettuce, shredded

Put 110 ml/4 fl oz of the water in a cup and sprinkle over the gelatine. Set aside for 5 minutes to soften and bring the remaining water to just below boiling point. Remove from the heat and stir in the gelatine, beating until it has dissolved. Reserve, but do not allow to set.

Decorate the egg halves with lumpfish roe. Brush with the prepared gelatine and put in a cool place to set.

Shell the lobsters and remove and reserve the legs. Slice the lobster meat into medallions. Place them on a rack over greaseproof paper and decorate with the truffles or olives. Brush with gelatine and put in a cool place to set.

Beat the remaining gelatine into the mayonnaise. Stir in the gherkins.

Cut a slice from the top of each tomato and reserve. With a teaspoon, carefully scoop out the flesh. Fill the tomato cases with shredded lettuce and the prepared mayonnaise. Set aside in a cool place.

Arrange the remaining lettuce on a large serving dish. Place the lobster medallions and reserved legs on top and fill the spaces in between with the decorated eggs and stuffed tomatoes. Serve with mayonnaise diluted with a little single cream, if liked.

CRAB GRATIN

Serves 6

1 large cooked crab
1 cooked lobster tail
50 ml/2 fl oz olive oil
1 onion, peeled and finely chopped
1 garlic clove, peeled and crushed
2 tbsp chopped parsley
8 tbsp tomato purée
4 tbsp puréed cooked or canned haricot beans
3 tbsp sherry
salt and freshly ground black pepper
75 g/3 oz breadcrumbs

Preheat the oven to 200° C/400° F, gas mark 6.

Detach the claws and legs and remove the meat from them and the shell. Chop finely and set aside. Scrub the shell.

Shell and chop the lobster tail and set aside.

Heat the oil and fry the onion and garlic for 5-8 minutes. Stir in half the parsley, the crabmeat, lobster meat and tomato purée. Cook for 5 minutes, stirring occasionally. Add the bean purée and the sherry and cook for 10 minutes. Season.

Stuff the shell with the crab mixture and sprinkle over the breadcrumbs and remaining parsley. Place the shell on a baking sheet and bake for 5 minutes, or until very hot.

Serve immediately.

**Below: Lobster Medallions
Below right: Curried Mussels (see page 50)**

SQUID IN ITS OWN INK

Serves 6

1.2 kg/2 lb squid
1-2 garlic bulbs, peeled
parsley sprigs
50 g/2 oz flour
75 ml/3 fl oz vegetable oil
300 ml/10 fl oz water
1 large onion, peeled and finely chopped
2 tbsp chopped parsley
salt

Clean the squid and reserve the ink sacs in cold water. Chop the tentacles and fins. Stuff each squid with the chopped fins and tentacles, 2 garlic cloves and 1 parsley sprig. Secure with cocktail sticks. Reserve 1 tsp of the flour and use the remainder to coat the squid. Heat the oil and fry the squid for 10 minutes. Drain.

Drain the ink sacs. Dissolve the ink in the water and set aside.

Fry the onion and chopped parsley in the oil for 5-8 minutes. Stir in the reserved flour and cook for 1 minute, stirring. Remove from the heat and stir in the ink. Return to the heat and bring to the boil, stirring. Season with salt and add the squid. Cover and cook over low heat for 15 minutes, or until the squid is tender.

Serve hot with fried bread shapes.

LANGOUSTINES VINAIGRETTE

Serves 6

1 kg/2 lb langoustines
salt and freshly ground white pepper
225 ml/8 fl oz olive oil
75 ml/3 fl oz white wine vinegar
2 hard-boiled eggs, shelled and chopped
1 onion, peeled and minced
1/2 tsp saffron threads
170 ml/6 fl oz brandy
pinch cayenne pepper

Cook the langoustines in well salted boiling water for 5-6 minutes. Set aside to cool in the water. Drain the langoustines, remove the heads and legs and peel. Cut the flesh into slices. Set aside in a shallow dish.

Beat together the oil and vinegar and season to taste. Add the eggs and the onion. Pound the saffron with a little salt in a mortar and add to the vinaigrette. Add the brandy and the cayenne pepper. Pour the vinaigrette over the langoustines and set aside to marinate in a cool place for 2-3 hours.

Serve decorated with the langoustine heads and legs.

CRAYFISH IN WHITE WINE

Serves 6

200 g/7 oz butter
1 carrot, peeled and chopped
1 onion, peeled and chopped
1 tbsp chopped parsley
1 bay leaf
2 tsp chopped thyme or 1/2 tsp dried thyme
200 ml/8 fl oz white wine
2 tbsp tomato purée
juice of 1 lemon
pinch cayenne pepper
salt and freshly ground white pepper
1 kg/2 lb cooked crayfish

Melt the butter and cook the carrot, onion, parsley, bay leaf and thyme for 5 minutes. Add the wine, bring to the boil and cook over high heat until reduced by about one-third.

Stir in the tomato purée and lemon juice and season with cayenne pepper, salt and white pepper. Add the crayfish, cover and cook for 10 minutes. If the sauce is drying out, add a little water.

Transfer to a large serving dish and serve immediately.

Top: Langoustines Vinaigrette
Bottom: Baby Eels Basque-style

GALICIAN SCALLOPS

Serves 6

12 scallops
juice of 2 lemons
salt
1 large onion, peeled and minced
200 g/7 oz ham, thinly sliced
2 hard-boiled eggs, shelled and chopped
6 tbsp breadcrumbs
2 tbsp chopped parsley
1 tsp paprika
coarse salt
110 g/4 oz butter, melted

Place the scallops in a low oven or on an electric hotplate, curved side downwards, for a few minutes to loosen. Using the point of a strong knife, prise open the shells. Separate the meat from the shells. Soak the scallops in cold water for 15 minutes and scrub the shells.

Preheat the oven to 200° C/400° F, gas mark 6.

Drain the scallops and pat dry. Sprinkle over the lemon juice and a little salt and arrange them in the half shells.

Mix together the onion, ham, eggs, breadcrumbs, parsley and paprika. Divide the mixture between the shells, covering the scallops completely.

Cover a baking sheet with a bed of coarse salt and arrange the shells, heaping the salt to prevent them from overturning. Drizzle over the butter and bake for 20 minutes, or until golden.

Serve immediately.

SUMMERTIME CRAYFISH

Serves 6

1 tbsp olive oil
1 onion, peeled and chopped
500 ml/17 fl oz white wine
1 parsley sprig
12 black peppercorns
salt
1 kg/2 lb crayfish

Heat the oil and sauté the onion. Add the wine, parsley, peppercorns and salt to taste and bring to the boil. Reduce the heat and simmer for 10 minutes.

Add the crayfish, cover and cook for 10 minutes. Remove the pan from the heat and set the crayfish aside to cool in the cooking liquid.

Drain the crayfish, transfer to a large serving plate and serve cold.

Top: Summertime Crayfish
Bottom: Galician Scallops

LOBSTER THERMIDOR

Serves 6

1 x 1 kg/2 lb live lobster
100 g/3 oz butter
225 ml/8 fl oz vegetable oil
salt and freshly ground black pepper
15 g/¹/₂ oz flour
200 ml/7 fl oz milk
1 small onion, peeled and finely chopped
250 ml/8 fl oz white wine
500 ml/17 fl oz double cream
1 tbsp chopped parsley
100 g/3 oz Parmesan cheese, grated
1 tbsp mustard

Preheat the oven to 180° C/350° F, gas mark 4.

Wrap one hand in a towel, Hold the lobster firmly and pierce the spot directly behind the head with the point of a sharp knife to kill it instantly. Cut it in half along the length of the body. Remove the gills, sac and intestine.

Melt 50 g/2 oz of the butter with the oil in a roasting tin. Place the lobster halves, cut side down in the tin and bake for 5 minutes.

Turn the lobster halves the other way up, season with salt and pepper and return to the oven for a further 15 minutes.

Melt 25 g/1 oz of the remaining butter and stir in the flour. Cook, stirring, for 1 minute. Remove the pan from the heat and gradually stir in the milk. Return the pan to the heat and bing to the boil, stirring. Simmer, stirring for 3-4 minutes, or until thick and smooth. Set aside.

Carefully remove the lobster meat from the half shells without breaking them. Dice the meat and set aside. Reserve the half shells.

Increase the oven temperature to 220°C /425° F, gas mark 7.

Melt the remaining butter and fry the onion for 5-8 minutes, or until golden. Add the wine and bring to the boil. Boil until reduced by about half. Stir in the cream, the white sauce and the parsley. Cook over low heat, stirring, until the sauce is smooth. Stir in the lobster meat and cook, stirring, for 5 minutes. Remove the pan from the heat.

Reserve 1-2 tbsp of the cheese and stir the remainder into the lobster mixture. Stir in the mustard. Pile the mixture into the two half shells and sprinkle over the remaining cheese. Cook in the oven for 5 minutes.

Arrange the lobster halves on a napkin on a large serving dish and serve immediately.

Lobster Thermidor

SCALLOPS GRATIN

Serves 4

8 scallops
75 g/3 oz butter
1 onion, peeled and finely chopped
250 ml/8 fl oz white wine
1 tsp chopped dill or ½ tsp dried dill
salt and freshly ground black pepper
6 tbsp breadcrumbs
6 tbsp tomato purée

Place the scallops in a low oven or on an electric hotplate, curved side down, for a few minutes. Prise open the shells with the point of a knife. Separate the meat from the shells and soak in cold water for 15 minutes. Scrub the shells and reserve. Drain the scallops, pat dry and set aside.

Preheat the grill.

Melt 25 g/ 1 oz of the butter and sauté the onion for 8-10 minutes. Add the scallops and wine, bring to the boil and allow to reduce by about one-third. Add the dill, season and cook for 1 minute.

Remove from the heat. Place the scallops on eight half shells. Cover with the tomato purée and sprinkle over the breadcrumbs. Melt the remaining butter and drizzle over. Grill for 5 minutes, or until very hot. Serve immediately.

PRAWNS IN GARLIC

Serves 6

100 ml/4 fl oz olive oil
1 chili pepper, seeded and sliced
3 garlic cloves, peeled and chopped
1 kg/2 lb prawns, peeled and deveined
½ tsp salt

Divide all the ingredients between six individual flameproof serving bowls and set aside to marinate for at least 1 hour.

About 10 minutes before serving, place the dishes on the heat and bring to the boil, stirring with a wooden spoon. When the oil is just about to boil, cover with a plate, remove from the heat and serve immediately.

SEAFOOD QUICHE

Serves 6

400 g/14 oz flour
salt
200 g/7 oz butter, diced
100 ml/4 fl oz water

Filling:
250 g/8oz shrimps, peeled and chopped
150 g/5 oz prawns, peeled and chopped
150 g/5 oz cooked lobster meat, sliced
500 ml/17 fl oz single cream
4 eggs
salt and freshly ground black pepper
6 langoustines or Mediterranean prawns

Preheat the oven to 200° C/400° F, gas mark 6.

Sift together the flour and salt. Rub in the butter until the mixture resembles fine breadcrumbs. Add the water and mix to form a dough. Turn out on to a lightly floured board and knead lightly until smooth. Roll out and line a 25 cm/10 in flan tin or six individual tartlet tins. Prick the base, fill with crumpled foil and bake blind for 12-14 minutes. Remove from the oven and set aside to cool.

Arrange the shrimps, prawns and lobster meat in the pastry case. Beat together the cream, eggs and seasoning and pour over. Bake for 25-30 minutes, or until set.

Serve hot or cold, garnished with the langoustines or Mediterranean prawns.

Left: Seafood Quiche
Right top: Prawns in Garlic
Right bottom: Scallops Gratin

SEAFOOD SALAD

Serves 6

400 g/14 oz white fish fillets
salt and freshly ground black pepper
1 kg/2 lb mussels
5 langoustines
500 g/1 lb shrimps, peeled and deveined
500 g/1 lb prawns, peeled and deveined
200 g/7 oz onions, peeled and finely chopped
2 red peppers, seeded and sliced
6 gherkins, sliced
75 g/3 oz capers
1 tsp chopped parsley

Dressing:
2 garlic cloves, peeled
salt
150 ml/5 fl oz olive oil
50 ml/2 fl oz white wine vinegar
3 hard-boiled eggs
1 tbsp chopped parsley

Place the fillets in a pan, cover with water and season. Bring to the boil, cover and simmer for 8-10 minutes, or until cooked.

Scrub the mussels under cold running water. Discard any that do not shut when sharply tapped. Place in a pan, cover with water and bring to the boil. Cook until the shells open.

Meanwhile, prepare and slice the langoustines and slice the shrimps and prawns. Set aside.

Drain the white fish, skin and chop. Set aside.

Drain the mussels and discard any shells that have not opened. Reserve a few mussels in their shells for the garnish. Remove the remainder from their shells and set aside.

Put the onions in a salad bowl and add the langoustines, shrimps, prawns, white fish, red peppers, gherkins and capers. .

To make the dressing, pound the garlic cloves with a little salt in a mortar. Beat together the oil, vinegar and pounded garlic until well mixed. Stir in the eggs and parsley.

Add the shelled mussels to the seafood salad and pour over the dressing. Toss gently so that it is thoroughly coated. Garnish with the reserved mussels and sprinkle over the parsley. Serve cold.

SEAFOOD CASSEROLE

Serves 6

250 g/8 oz langoustines
250 g/8 oz spiny lobsters (langoustes)
500 g/1 lb prawns
500 g/1 lb clams

25 ml/1 fl oz vegetable oil
1 onion, peeled and finely chopped
3 garlic cloves, peeled and finely chopped
500 g/1 lb crabmeat
salt and freshly ground black pepper
1/4 tsp saffron threads
1 tbsp tomato purée
1/2 tsp paprika
1 tbsp chopped parsley

Peel the langoustines, lobsters and prawns, cut in slices and set and set aside. Place the shells in a pan with a little water and bring to the boil. Simmer for 10 minutes.

Scrub the clams under cold running water. Discard any that do not shut when sharply tapped. Place them in a pan, cover with water and bring to the boil. Cook until the shells open.

Strain the shellfish stock and reserve. Drain the clams. Discard any that have not opened. Reserve the cooking liquid. Remove one shell from each clam. Combine the stock and the cooking liquid from the clams and strain through clean muslin to remove any grit. Set aside.

Heat the oil in a flameproof casserole and fry the onion and garlic for 5-8 minutes. Add the crabmeat, 100 ml/ 4 fl oz of the mixed stock and salt and pepper. Cook for 5 minutes.

Pound the saffron with a little salt in a mortar. Add to the crab mixture and stir in the tomato purée, paprika and parsley. Add the reserved langoustines, lobsters, prawns and clams and pour over the remaining mixed stock. Cook for 8-10 minutes, or until thoroughly heated through.

Serve immediately in the casserole.

LANGOUSTINE RING

Serves 6

750 g/1 lb langoustines
10 black peppercorns
salt
1 bay leaf
500 ml/17 fl oz water
500 g/1 lb potatoes, peeled
200 g/7 oz peas, shelled
200 g/7 oz green beans, trimmed
200 g/7 oz carrots, peeled
110 ml/4 fl oz mayonnaise
1 envelope gelatine

Put the langoustines in a large pan, cover with water and add the peppercorns, a little salt and the bay leaf. Bring to the boil and cook for 2 minutes. Drain and place in a bowl of lightly salted, cold water. Peel the langoustines and set aside. Put the shells in a pan with the water, bring to the

boil and simmer for 20 minutes. Strain the fish stock and set aside.

Cook the potatoes in plenty of boiling, salted water for 20-25 minutes, or until tender. Drain and set aside to cool.

Cook the peas in lightly salted, boiling water for 15-20 minutes, or until tender. Drain and set aside to cool.

Cook the beans in boiling water for 10 minutes. Add a little salt and cook for a further 5 minutes, or until tender but still crisp. Drain and refresh with cold water. Set aside.

Cook the carrots in boiling salted water for 10-15 minutes, or until tender. Drain and set aside to cool.

When the vegetables are cold, dice the potatoes, beans and carrots and mix them together. Add the peas and stir in the mayonnaise. Set aside.

Put a little fish stock in a cup and sprinkle over the gelatine. Set aside for 5 minutes to soften and bring the remaining stock to the boil. Remove the stock from the heat and add the gelatine, stirring until it has dissolved.

Coat the inside of a ring mould with a thin layer of gelatine, making sure it is completely covered. Arrange the langoustines in the mould and top with the vegetable mixture. Cover with the remaining gelatine. (If there is more gelatine than is required, it can be chilled in a shallow dish and, when set, chopped and used as a garnish.)

When the gelatine is cold, cover the mould place it in the refrigerator for 2 hours, or until set.

To serve, quickly dip the mould in hot water and invert on to a serving plate.

SPIDER CRAB CREAM

Serves 4

5 litres/8 pints water
1 carrot, peeled
1 onion, peeled
100 ml/4 fl oz vinegar
coarse salt
10 sprigs parsley
1 bay leaf
5 sprigs thyme
1 spider crab
75 g/ 3 oz breadcrumbs

Sauce:
100 g/3 oz butter
75 g/3 oz flour
500 ml/17 fl oz milk
salt and freshly ground white pepper
3 egg yolks
100 ml/4 fl oz double cream

Put the water, carrot, onion, vinegar, salt, parsley, bay leaf and thyme in a large pan and bring to the boil. Add the crab, cover and cook for 30 minutes.

Drain the crab and set aside to cool. Once the crab is cold, break off the legs and remove the crabmeat without damaging the shell. Cut in slices and reserve. Scrub the shell and reserve.

Preheat the grill.

To make the sauce, melt the butter, add the flour and cook, stirring, for 2 minutes.

Remove from the heat and gradually stir in the milk. Return to the heat and bring to the boil, stirring. Cook, stirring, for 2-3 minutes, until thick and smooth.

Remove from the heat and season. Beat together the egg yolks and cream and then beat the mixture into the sauce.

Stir the crabmeat, and any juices released as it was cut up, into the sauce. Pile the mixture into the shell, sprinkle over the breadcrumbs. Grill for 5 minutes, or until very hot. Serve immediately.

Spider Crab Cream

INDEX